Cambridge Elements

Elements in Ethics
edited by
Ben Eggleston
University of Kansas
Dale E. Miller
Old Dominion University, Virginia

UTILITARIANISM

Tim Mulgan

University of St Andrews and University of Auckland

CAMBRIDGE
UNIVERSITY PRESS

CAMBRIDGE
UNIVERSITY PRESS

University Printing House, Cambridge CB2 8BS, United Kingdom

One Liberty Plaza, 20th Floor, New York, NY 10006, USA

477 Williamstown Road, Port Melbourne, VIC 3207, Australia

314–321, 3rd Floor, Plot 3, Splendor Forum, Jasola District Centre,
New Delhi – 110025, India

79 Anson Road, #06–04/06, Singapore 079906

Cambridge University Press is part of the University of Cambridge.

It furthers the University's mission by disseminating knowledge in the pursuit of
education, learning, and research at the highest international levels of excellence.

www.cambridge.org
Information on this title: www.cambridge.org/9781108730600
DOI: 10.1017/9781108582643

First published 2020

A catalogue record for this publication is available from the British Library.

ISBN 978-1-108-73060-0 Paperback
ISSN 2516-4031 (online)
ISSN 2516-4023 (print)

Utilitarianism

Elements in Ethics

DOI: 10.1017/9781108582643
First published online: January 2020

Tim Mulgan
University of St Andrews and University of Auckland

Author for correspondence: Tim Mulgan, tpm6@st-andrews.ac.uk

Abstract: Utilitarians identify morality with the impartial promotion of well-being. This Element asks how utilitarianism might develop in possible futures broken by climate change or transformed by new technologies. It argues that concern for future people should dominate our ethical thinking, that an adequate utilitarian future ethic must be collective and pessimistic, and that future utilitarians must think imaginatively about the nature of well-being, the value of possible future populations, and the threat of human extinction. Utilitarianism is presented as a living ethical tradition, not an abstract set of timeless principles or a purely historical artefact.

Keywords: Utilitarianism, Future Ethics, Moral Philosophy

ISBNs: 9781108730600 (PB), 9781108582643 (OC)
ISSNs: 2516-4031 (online), 2516-4023 (print)

Contents

1 Introducing Utilitarianism

Utilitarianism is a historical tradition in moral and political thought. Although utilitarian themes are present in all philosophical schools – throughout the Western tradition since the Ancient Greeks, and also in early Chinese and Indian thought – modern utilitarianism is especially associated with three thinkers active in Britain between the late eighteenth and late nineteenth centuries: Jeremy Bentham (1748–1832), John Stuart Mill (1806–73), and Henry Sidgwick (1838–1900). Utilitarianism was a dominant mode of ethical thinking in Western philosophy in the early twentieth century. Although less dominant today, it remains very influential.

This Element is neither a historical account of the utilitarian tradition nor a standard textbook introduction to contemporary utilitarianism. Several other books already fill those niches admirably.[1] Instead, this Element explores the future of utilitarianism, asking where utilitarians' perennial preoccupations might lead in various possible futures. Section 1 introduces the utilitarian tradition and the approach taken in this Element. Section 2 argues that, in our present circumstances, the future should dominate our ethical thinking and that any adequate utilitarian future ethic will be collective and pessimistic. Section 3 outlines contemporary debates about the content and scope of well-being and asks how those debates might be transformed across a range of different possible futures. Section 4 addresses a number of puzzles in contemporary future ethics – especially Parfit's Repugnant Conclusion and Non-Identity Problem, asymmetries in procreative ethics, the destabilising impact of empirical and normative uncertainty, and existential threats of human extinction.

Any account of a tradition as rich and varied as utilitarianism is bound to be controversial. My aim here is not to defend any detailed exegesis (either historical or contemporary) but rather to draw out some central utilitarian themes. The defining feature of utilitarianism is that it bases its moral evaluations on *impartial promotion of well-being*. (As we'll see, different utilitarians evaluate different things: acts, rules, moral codes, social institutions.) Impartiality, promotion, well-being: these three key terms need unpacking. I explore promotion in section 2.2 and well-being in section 3. I begin with impartiality and its implications.

Utilitarians are committed to *impartiality*. In the famous phrase attributed to Jeremy Bentham: 'Everyone to count for one, and nobody for more than one.'[2]

---

[1] Good introductory textbooks on utilitarianism include Bykvist, 2009; de Lazari-Radek and Singer, 2017; Mulgan, 2007; Shaw, 1999. An excellent contemporary overview is Eggleston and Miller, 2014. An excellent recent historical overview is Schultz, 2017.

[2] The attribution goes back to Mill, 1963, vol. 10, p. 257. While it is often attributed to Bentham, this precise phrase is apparently not found in any of his extant writings. Perhaps the closest

Human well-being is equally valuable no matter whose it is. Following Bentham, utilitarians emphasise impartiality as a counterweight to the perennial threat of *egoism*. This threat is both practical and theoretical. We must guard against our natural tendency to give undue weight to our own interests, values, traditions, or perspectives or to *believe* what suits our interests, aligns our duties with our inclinations, confirms our prejudices, or otherwise enables us to think well of ourselves. As a result, utilitarians are especially suspicious of moral principles that allow us to privilege our own interests.

Many moral theories agree that we should treat persons impartially. (Indeed, many philosophers have built impartiality into the very definition of the 'moral point of view'. See, e.g., Baier, 1958; Hare, 1982.) But utilitarians go further in two ways. First, utilitarians are impartial between species – or, more generally, between *kinds* of beings for whom things can go well. Well-being is defined without reference to any particular species – in particular, without special reference to *Homo sapiens*. It is then an empirical question whether or not non-human animals matter. For instance, if – as hedonists argue – well-being is pleasure and the absence of pain, then all sentient animals matter, and they matter in exactly the same way as human beings.[3] This feature of utilitarian impartiality has notoriously radical implications for our treatment of animals. (It is not a coincidence that many leading figures in the animal liberation movement are utilitarians. See especially Singer, 1975.) I argue below that future utilitarians may face analogous challenges relating to the well-being of extra-terrestrial organisms or digital beings. And, as we shall see throughout this Element, the underlying commitment to impartiality has many other implications for utilitarian future ethics.

Modern philosophical utilitarianism comes in a bewildering variety of forms. We can illustrate these by starting with the following basic formulation.

Hedonist Act Utilitarianism (HAU): The right act in any situation is the act that maximises expected total net pleasure (i.e., the balance of pleasure over pain).

Although it appears simple, we can break HAU down into ten component claims:

---

approximation is the following passage from Bentham's *Rationale of Judicial Evidence*: 'every individual in the country tells for one; no individual for more than one.' (Bentham, 1838, vol. 7, p. 334.)

[3] Hedonists could still regard human well-being as more significant, but only insofar as humans are capable of greater heights of enjoyment or greater depths of suffering than animals. A human's pleasure in listening to a symphony or terror in the face of imminent torture might simply be greater than anything a spider can experience. But if the spider could appreciate Mozart, its pleasure would count as much as ours! We return to hedonism in section 3.1 and to animal welfare in section 3.2.

1 **Consequentialism:** Utilitarians insist that well-being is valuable. But there are many different ways to respond to the belief that something is valuable. Should we *honour* what is valuable? (Treating its instances with respect, reverence, or worship; seeking to protect or preserve them.) Or should we try to *embody* or *instantiate* particular values? (Should utilitarians recognise the value of happiness by seeking to be happy?) Consequentialists argue that we should *promote* value by aiming to bring about valuable outcomes. Contemporary moral philosophy treats utilitarianism as a species of consequentialism. In this Element, I will largely follow this assumption. However, I often question specific consequentialist claims, and in section 4.3 I explore explicitly non-consequentialist forms of utilitarianism.

2 **Welfarism:** Outcome value is determined exclusively by the welfare of individuals. (Alternatives include ecological values and perfectionist values.)

3 **Hedonism:** Individual welfare is determined exclusively by pleasure and pain. (Alternatives include preference satisfaction and objective goods.)

Consequentialism tells us to promote value, welfarism identifies value with optimal well-being, and hedonism delivers a metric for *the value of individual lives*. HAU then aggregates individual value along three dimensions: persons, times, and prospects (cf. Broome, 2004).

4 **Totalism:** Outcome value is determined by total welfare. (Alternative measures include average welfare and the distribution of welfare.)

5 **Temporal Neutrality:** The contribution that an individual life makes to the value of an outcome does *not* depend on when that life is lived. (Alternatives include temporal discounting and other temporally asymmetrical views.)

Aggregating across persons and times gives us a measure of *outcome value*. To measure the value of *acts*, HAU then aggregates over prospects.

6 **Expectation:** The value of an act is the sum of the value of each prospective outcome multiplied by the probability of that outcome occurring if the act is performed. (Alternatives include risk-aversion or risk-seeking.)

Having ranked acts according to their value, HAU then tells us how we should *respond* to act values:

7 **Maximisation:** The right act is the one with the greatest (expected) value. (The main alternative is *satisficing*, where agents are permitted to choose any act whose (expected) value is 'good enough'.)

Finally, HAU's initial decision to focus on *acts* itself combines three controversial claims:

8 **Act Focus:** The primary focus of consequentialist evaluation is acts. (Alternative foci include rules, motives, codes, outlooks, dispositions, institutions, constitutions, beliefs, etc.)

9 **Direct Evaluation:** We evaluate each act directly in terms of its consequences. (The alternative is to evaluate one unit *indirectly* in terms of a second unit chosen because of *its* (direct) consequences. For instance, rule consequentialism first directly evaluates codes of rules and then uses the optimal code to indirectly evaluate acts.)

10 **Individual:** The primary focus of consequentialist evaluation is the particular acts of an individual agent. (The main alternative is the collective evaluation of sets of acts performed by groups of agents.)

Each of these ten claims is a site of ongoing controversy within contemporary moral philosophy. Some claims are regarded as *essential* to utilitarianism. For instance, utilitarianism is often *defined* as the set of possible theories that combine consequentialism and welfarism. And, as I said at the outset, temporal neutrality is often regarded as a central utilitarian commitment. Rejecting any of these three components would amount to a rejection of utilitarianism per se. But that still leaves seven components: hedonism, totalism, expectation, maximisation, act focus, direct evaluation, and individual evaluation. Rejecting any of these claims counts as a move *within* utilitarianism.

I set maximisation and expectation aside for now. (I return to them briefly in sections 4.5 and 4.6.) I will focus on three remaining contested aspects of the utilitarian response to value.

1 **Individual welfare:** Is hedonism the correct account of well-being?
2 **Aggregation:** Is totalism the best way to go from the value of individual lives to the value of outcomes?
3 **Promotion:** Once we have ordered possible outcomes by their value, how should we respond? What is our focus of evaluation (acts, motives, rules)? And should we evaluate that item directly or indirectly, individually or collectively?

I address well-being and aggregation in sections 3 and 4.1 respectively. However, for reasons that will emerge as we proceed, I begin with the third set of questions.

2 A New Utilitarianism: Future-Oriented, Collective, Pessimistic

2.1 Why the Future Should Dominate Utilitarian Thinking

Utilitarians have long argued that our obligations to distant strangers are more onerous than most of us assume. We cannot discount well-being just because it happens a long way away. Our obligations to distant future people are, if anything, ever more pressing than what we owe to present distant strangers. Our relations with distant future people are integral to our own moral community – and arguably to our present projects and achievements. Also, our impact on future people *includes the content of their moral outlook*. These connections will be a central theme of this Element.

Up until the late twentieth century, like most other moral philosophers, utilitarians focused primarily on obligations to contemporaries and/or people in the near future. This can seem surprising, because utilitarians have always recognised that the well-being of even the most distant future people is as important as our own. The general utilitarian commitment to impartiality extends to *temporal impartiality*. Human well-being is equally valuable no matter whose it is – *or when they live*. For utilitarians, the interests of future people count as much as those of present people. In other words, utilitarians reject *pure temporal discounting*.

The practice of discounting future harms and benefits is relatively uncontroversial as a proxy for uncertainty – or to accommodate the remote possibility that there will be no future people. (Humanity might be wiped out by an unpreventable asteroid strike, for instance.) There are also sound utilitarian reasons to discount the future *if* you are confident that future people will be richer than present people or that technological advances will leave them better able to exploit any valuable resource. (Of course, as we shall see, this argument is reversed if we expect future people to be worse off.) The controversial philosophical question is whether we should apply pure temporal discounting, where future happiness counts for less simply *because* it lies in the future. One common justification is that this pure time preference mirrors actual behaviour. We do discount future benefits both to ourselves and to others.

Discount rates have a huge practical impact. Climate change provides a striking illustration. One prominent sceptical argument holds that the *future* benefit of preventing climate change is not worth the *present* cost. We could do more good by devoting our present resources to the alleviation of present poverty. Even a modest discount of 5 per cent per annum makes it 'uneconomic' to spend even one dollar today to avert a global catastrophe in five hundred years' time. (To be worth spending a dollar today, the catastrophe has to cost $137,466,652,006 at that future date.) Different economists reach radically different conclusions on the basis of their divergent discount rates. (Compare, e.g., Stern, 2006 and Nordhaus, 2007, pp. 143–61.)

While pure time preferences are controversial among economists, most utilitarian *moral philosophers* reject them and embrace temporal impartiality (Cowen and Parfit, 1992). Unlike some non-utilitarians (e.g., Heyd, 1992), utilitarians cannot simply set future ethics aside. So why did utilitarians ignore the distant future despite recognising that distant future people are just as important?

Earlier utilitarians sidelined the future for three main reasons: *optimism*, *similarity*, and *convergence*. Like other philosophers, they assumed (1) that future people will be better off than present people, (2) that the future will resemble the present in most morally relevant ways, and (3) that the interests of present and future people largely converge. Environmental crises and other recent developments undermine all three presuppositions. We must now recognise that future people might be worse off than ourselves, that they might inhabit very unfamiliar futures, and that their interests might conflict with our own. Utilitarians must now pay special attention to future ethics.

Traditional moral and political philosophy often presumes an *affluent future* that resembles the past in most morally significant ways, with the exception that future people will be better off than us. In particular, it is assumed that future societies enjoy what John Rawls calls 'favourable conditions' (Rawls, 1971, p. 178), where it is possible to establish liberal democratic institutions that meet all basic needs without sacrificing any basic liberties. And Rawls argues that if such institutions *are* established, then we can expect to see modest increases in living standards across generations. What is best for us is thus also good for our descendants.

An affluent future is possible. But it is not inevitable. In my book *Ethics for a Broken World*, I imagine a future broken by climate change, where a chaotic climate makes life precarious, each generation is worse off than the last, it is no longer possible to meet everyone's basic needs, and our affluent way of life is no longer an option (Mulgan, 2011, 2014a, 2015b, 2015c, 2015d, 2016, 2017, 2018a, 2018b, 2018c).

This broken future is *credible*. No one can reasonably be confident that it won't happen. It involves no outlandish claims, scientific impossibilities, or implausible expectations about human behaviour. Climate change – or some other disaster – might produce a broken future. I argue in sections 3.4 and 3.5 that even some of the brightest-looking futures have a potentially (very) broken flipside.

The credibility of the broken future undermines our three presumptions of optimism, similarity, and convergence. In a broken future, people are (by definition) worse off than ourselves. As I argue below, their moral challenges differ from our own. Finally, both the likelihood and the severity of the broken future may depend on *present* choices. In particular, we might be able to mitigate future brokenness by making present sacrifices. If so, present and future interests conflict – and one key task for future ethics is to balance these competing interests.

Of course, while it is credible, the broken future is not inevitable. The future might be much better or much worse. Affluent liberal society promises to meet all basic needs but not to satisfy all desires. Once basic needs and basic liberties are guaranteed, the primary focus of our affluent theories of justice is the distribution of resources that remain scarce *relative to desires*. In the broken world, the affluent promise is broken: not all basic needs can be met. At the other extreme lies the promise of a *post-scarcity* future where resources are not scarce even relative to anyone's desires (Mulgan, 2017). Like the broken future, this other extreme possibility cannot be ruled out.

It is tempting to assume that post-scarcity futures are ethically uninteresting. However, this is too quick an assumption. In a post-scarcity world, it is *possible* to simultaneously satisfy all desires. It does not follow that this happens automatically or permanently. Post-scarcity conflict is still possible for several reasons. First, powerful individuals whose desires are all *already* satisfied might oppose a new system designed to satisfy everyone else's desires as well. Why take the risk? (Post-scarcity technology, if concentrated in a few hands, might enable the few to easily dominate the many.) Second, people may reasonably disagree about how post-scarcity life should be organised. And we cannot dismiss such disagreements as trivial matters of taste. On any account of human well-being other than crude actual-present-desire-maximisation, some possible post-scarcity scenarios are (very much) better than others. It is good (other things being equal) if all desires are satisfied. But it also matters what those satisfied desires are *for*. Imagine a post-scarcity paradise where nanotech-nology has produced 'cornucopia machines' capable of re-assembling air mole-cules to create any desired object (Stross, 2005). We can still ask what people will *do* with their cornucopia machines. Will they all descend into a drug-induced stupor or retreat into mindless virtual realities? (What do present people do with the potentially infinite resources of the World Wide Web?) Will anyone have the incentive or the drive to invent or explore *new* patterns to programme into cornucopia machines or new ways to spend their (now effectively limitless) leisure time? Cautionary tales of wishes granted by duplicitous literal-minded genies, Asimov-literal robots, and other post-scarcity fictions teach us that a world where everyone gets what they want could be shallow, unstable, or otherwise very grim. (In Stross, 2005, for instance, the arrival of cornucopia machines escalates existing social tensions into an all-out civil war.) Finally, unless we imagine beings with radically non-human desires, our post-scarcity world cannot literally involve everyone getting everything they want. People's strongest desires often ineliminably involve other people. And those desires inevitably conflict. (Consider Hobbesian desires for power or pre-eminence, the never-ending consumerist urge to keep up with the Joneses, or the desire for a reciprocal and exclusive romantic relationship.) Once again, it matters how these post-scarcity conflicts are resolved.

We simply have no idea what the distant future will be like. Pervasive uncertainty is another reason why future ethics is so challenging. If we knew *which* future would emerge, perhaps we could plan for it – focusing all our philosophical energy on resolving the questions that most matter *in that particular future*. But the possible futures are many, their comparative value is hard to discern, and each new generation will face its own new menu of possible futures. The central utilitarian ethical task is thus to enable future people to think creatively about the even-more-distant possible worlds that lie in *their* future. And we can only accomplish that task by thinking imaginatively about those futures ourselves and teaching our immediate successors to do likewise.

Uncertainty is a general problem for utilitarians. Taking the distant future seriously obviously exacerbates this problem. Our uncertainty about the future is not only empirical. It is often also normative. We can distinguish at least three dimensions of normative uncertainty: (1) we don't know what normative questions will loom largest for future people (and therefore we don't know how best to prepare them for the ethical challenges they will face), (2) we don't know what answers future people will give to those normative questions (and therefore we cannot easily predict their behaviour), and (3) we don't know what *actually* matters (and therefore we don't know whether some present choice would make things better or worse for future people). Our ignorance of future people's questions and answers exacerbates our ignorance of what the future will be like. But we also don't know whether or not any *particular* future would be *desirable*.

Utilitarians should pay particular attention to futures that are *credible, unsettling*, and *worrying*: futures that might happen, that destabilise the presuppositions of our current ethical thinking, and that raise very significant ethical challenges for future people.

As well as broken futures, I will explore moral challenges associated with some specific *technological* futures:

- *Virtual futures* where people have abandoned the real world altogether and spend their entire lives plugged into an experience machine that perfectly simulates any possible human experience (Nozick, 1974, pp. 42–5).
- *Digital futures* where flesh-and-blood humans are joined – or even *replaced* – by digital beings – intelligent machines and/or digital copies of human brains (see, e.g., Blackford and Broderick, 2014; Bostrom, 2014; Hauskeller, 2013, pp. 115–32; Mulgan, 2014a, 2016, forthcoming b).
- *Extraterrestrial futures* where some, most, or all future well-being is enjoyed by beings who do not inhabit the Earth. These extraterrestrial beings might be

(1) human beings spread through the solar system; inhabiting domes on Mars, the moon, or other solar bodies; travelling between the stars; or colonising distant exoplanets; (2) our distant trans-human or non-human descendants (perhaps uploaded into fully digital worlds); (3) the distant descendants of some other terrestrial species who turn out to be more robust than humans; or (4) the 'indigenous' inhabitants of some extraterrestrial environment.

Virtual, digital, and extraterrestrial futures are all credible (Mulgan, 2014a, 2018a, 2018b, 2018c). No one can reasonably assume they won't happen. Also, although they are often presented as *alternatives* to the broken future – as ways to sidestep future scarcity – these futures can also be very broken themselves. (And, crucially, as soon as we try to *evaluate* technological futures, we encounter a host of contested questions in utilitarian value theory and metaphysics.)

These possible futures are all *inhabited*. Each contains individuals whose well-being matters.[4] But we cannot simply assume that the future – especially the distant future – will be inhabited at all. Utilitarians must also consider *empty futures* devoid of creatures whose lives can go well or ill. Credible threats of human extinction make empty futures more salient than ever before. This introduces new utilitarian questions. In particular: is the *expected value* of an inhabited future positive or negative? If we must choose between empty and inhabited futures, which should we prefer?

Future ethics raises urgent new challenges. One final reason for utilitarians to focus on future ethics is the division of intellectual labour. What ultimately matters is not the importance of the question but what we can add by our contribution to it. Moral relations between affluent contemporaries have been studied extensively. While it is radical in practice, the utilitarian view of those relations is fairly familiar. It is in the new territory of future ethics that individual utilitarian thinkers (and individual books) can get the biggest bang for their philosophical buck.

2.2 Why Utilitarian Future Ethics Must Be Collective

Act utilitarianism tells us that the right act in any situation is whatever produces the best outcome. Utilitarians can depart from this orthodox position in three ways (Eggleston, 2014; Miller, 2014; Driver, 2014):

1 **Alternative foci of evaluation:** Instead of focusing on acts, we could evaluate rules, motives, dispositions, moral outlooks, social institutions, etc. We might seek the optimal rule or motive rather than the optimal act.

---

[4] One possible exception, as I argue below, is that it is not obvious that all digital futures are really inhabited.

2 **Indirect evaluation:** Instead of assessing acts directly, we could assess them indirectly. Perhaps the right act is whatever follows from the optimal rule or motive.
3 **Collective evaluation:** Instead of asking how each individual agent can make the world better, collective utilitarianism focuses instead on what we do together.

Most introductions to utilitarianism treat act utilitarianism as the natural default position (e.g., Bykvist, 2009; de Lazari-Radek and Singer, 2017). My approach in this Element is different. I will argue that, whatever its general merits in other contexts, individual evaluation is not the best place to begin our exploration of *future* ethics. In this section, I explore three utilitarian departures from individual direct act utilitarianism: Parfit's emphasis on what we together do, Hooker's rule utilitarianism, and my own ideal outlook utilitarianism. These introduce, respectively: a shift from individual to collective evaluation; a shift from direct evaluation of acts to indirect evaluation of acts in terms of rules, motives, or outlooks; and a focus on the moral outlook that we should teach to future generations. Each of these departures is controversial. However, they collectively offer utilitarian future ethics new and under-explored resources.

2.2.1 Parfit on What We Together Do

Our most pressing intergenerational dilemmas are large-scale, long-term collective action problems. (It makes little sense for any one individual agent to ask: 'What can *I* do about climate change?') In 1984, Derek Parfit warned that focusing on the isolated effects of individual actions can blind us to the very real and harmful impacts of 'what we together do' (Parfit, 1984, chapter 3). In cases where the impact of each individual's actions is negligible or even imperceptible, we may fail to even recognise that we are *collectively* inflicting enormous harm on future people. Perhaps the best way for *me* to promote well-being is to amass a vast fortune by emitting fossil fuels and then donate the profits to charity. If so, a consistent act utilitarian would applaud such behaviour. But if we all reason this way, the results may be disastrous. Humanity's failure to diagnose – let alone solve – the myriad collective action problems of contemporary environmentalism suggests that Parfit was right.

Parfit identifies five common 'mistakes in moral mathematics' (Parfit, 1984, p. 66). Parfit argues that these mistakes arise because we focus on the direct effects of particular actions while ignoring the systemic impact of collective patterns of behaviour. The most significant mistakes, for our present purposes, are the third, fourth, and fifth: ignoring small chances, small effects, and imperceptible effects.

Parfit illustrates these mistakes using a number of striking examples. Here are two of them:

> *How the Fishermen Cause a Disaster*: There are many fishermen, who earn their living by fishing separately on some large lake. If each fisherman does not restrict his catch, he will catch within the next few seasons more fish. But he will thereby lower the total catch by a much larger number. Since there are many fishermen, if each does not restrict his catch, he will only trivially affect the number caught by each of the others. The fishermen believe that such trivial effects can be morally ignored. Because they believe this, even though they never do what they believe to be wrong, they do not restrict their catches. Each thereby increases his own catch, but causes a much greater lowering in the total catch. Because they all act in this way, the result is a disaster. After a few seasons, all catch very many fewer fish. They cannot feed themselves or their children. (Parfit, 1984, p. 84.)

> *The Commuter's Dilemma*: Suppose that we live in the suburbs of a large city. We can get to and return from work either by car or by bus. Since there are no bus-lanes, extra traffic slows buses just as much as it slows cars. We could therefore know the following to be true. When most of us are going by car, if any one of us goes by car rather than by bus, he will thereby save himself some time, but he will impose on others a much greater total loss of time. This effect would be dispersed. Each might cause a hundred others to be delayed for twenty seconds, or cause a thousand others to be delayed for two seconds. Most of us would regard such effects as so trivial that they can be morally ignored. We would then believe that even a rational altruist can justifiably choose to go by car rather than by bus. But if most of us make this choice we shall all be delayed for a long time every day. (Parfit, 1984, p. 85.)

In both cases, Parfit argues that *rational altruists* (who care impartially about promoting everyone's best interests) can only avoid these bad results by appealing not to the effects of what each person does but to 'the effect of what all together do' (Parfit, 1984, p. 85). Parfit's conclusion is worth quoting at length:

> As conditions change, we may need to make some changes in the way we think about morality. ... Common-Sense Morality works best in small communities. ... Until this century, most of mankind lived in small communities. What each did could affect only a few others. But conditions have now changed. Each of us can now, in countless ways, affect countless other people. We can have real though small effects on thousands or millions of people. ... It is not enough to ask, 'Will my act harm other people?' Even if the answer is No, my act may still be wrong, *because* of its effect on other people. I should ask, 'Will my act be one of a set of acts that will *together* harm other people?' (Parfit, 1984, pp. 85–6.)

Within utilitarianism, Parfit's recommended shift in moral perspective leads from individual evaluation to collective evaluation. This connects with an emerging theme in climate change ethics. Individual moral reasoning – whether utilitarian or not – is especially ill-equipped to deal with the ethical challenges of climate change. Similarly, the consequentialist environmental philosopher Robin Attfield distinguishes between *pre-modern ethics*, which dealt with 'direct responsibility', and *modern ethics*, which must deal with 'mediated responsibility' (Attfield, 2009).

The following pair of contrasting examples nicely illustrate Attfield's distinction between direct and mediated responsibility:

1 **Car Crash:** I drive my car recklessly and hit person A, breaking their arm.
2 **Climate Change:** Along with millions of others, I drive my car. This contributes to higher CO_2 levels, which contribute to higher global temperatures, which extend the geographical reach of malaria parasites, which leads to person B contracting malaria in some future century.

Car Crash is a clear case of *direct* responsibility. An individual action has a clear and definite effect on an identifiable present victim. I break A's arm. Climate Change is a clear case of *mediated* responsibility. We are now dealing with the very indirect uncertain impact of a collective pattern of behaviour (involving many millions of present and future people) on some unidentifiable distant future person who might not ever have existed at all under any other collective pattern of behaviour. It is very hard to say what, if anything, *I* have done to B (cf. Sinnott-Armstrong, 2005).

2.2.2 Hooker's Rule Utilitarianism

Many collective utilitarians combine Parfit's emphasis on collective responsibility with a second shift to an *indirect* evaluation of acts. For instance, in Brad Hooker's influential rule utilitarianism (hereafter 'Hooker's RU'), the right action is whatever follows from the set of rules whose internalisation by everyone would produce the best consequences (Hooker, 2000, p. 32).[5] Hooker's RU pictures morality as a collective enterprise, and it evaluates moral codes by their collective impact on human well-being. Its fundamental moral questions are: 'What if *we* did that?' and 'How should *we* live?' Hooker's RU is a two-stage theory. We first identify the *ideal moral code* and then we assess acts *indirectly*: the right act is the act that would be performed by someone who had internalised that code.

---

[5] Hooker calls his theory *rule consequentialism*, because his foundational values combine total welfare with fairness. Because our present focus is on the promotion of value rather than the substantive content of value, I focus here on a simpler rule utilitarianism version. (I also simplify Hooker's view in other ways. For a full discussion, see Mulgan, 2006, pp. 130–60, 2015b, 2017.)

Rule utilitarianism chooses moral rules on the basis of what would happen if everybody adopted those rules. One obvious objection is that this leads to undesirable results under conditions of *partial compliance* where not everyone conforms to the rule in question. Consider two examples:

- **Sucker:** The rule utilitarian ideal code prohibits theft, assault, fraud and dishonesty. Therefore, people living in a world where everyone always follows the ideal code will never lock their doors (or even have lockable doors), always loan money to anyone who promises to repay them, always click on email links and attachments, believe everything they are told, never consider anyone a threat to their personal safety, and so on. But it would be crazy to behave like this in the real world.
- **Counterproductive:** Several people are drowning in the surf. I am one of several bystanders. If we all co-operate, we could save everyone using a nearby boat. However, no one can operate the boat on their own. Each of us could also save one person from drowning if we act alone. I know that none of the other bystanders will help and that there is nothing I can do to persuade them. However, as a loyal rule utilitarian, I follow the 'optimal rule' and (pointlessly) play my part in the optimal pattern of behaviour by trying to launch the boat single-handedly.

Rule utilitarians introduce two changes to avoid these two objections:

- **Retreat from universality:** Instead of idealising to full compliance, we ask what would happen if *nearly everyone* followed a particular set of rules. This enables us to capture the idea that any acceptable moral code must respond to the fact that, in any realistic human situation, there will be some people who depart from the ideal code.
- **Disaster avoidance clauses:** The optimal rules include clauses of the following form: 'Do x, unless doing x will lead to great disaster because everyone else is not doing x, in which case do whatever is necessary to avoid disaste.' (Hooker, 2000, pp. 98–9, 133–6.)

Unfortunately, the introduction of disaster avoidance clauses leads directly to another objection: that rule utilitarianism *collapses* into act utilitarianism. Once we allow some departures from the ideal rules, where do we stop? As utilitarians, shouldn't we extend our disaster avoidance clause to cover any failure to maximise the good? But then our ideal code will consist of rules of infinite complexity telling people to maximise utility in each particular situation – at which point it is more efficient to simply replace it with the single act utilitarian rule: 'Do whatever best promotes well-being.'

The best rule utilitarian response to this objection begins with a more general objection to utilitarianism. Opponents often accuse utilitarianism of departing too radically from common sense morality. Utilitarian agents, it is argued, will torture children, condemn the innocent, violate the most basic rights, or demand the most extreme sacrifices whenever doing so will best promote aggregate happiness. Rule utilitarians argue that they are better placed to rebut this objection than act utilitarians because they can offer a moderate, liberal utilitarian theory. Drawing on arguments made famous by J. S. Mill – and before him by William Paley, who argued that God instituted morality to promote human well-being – rule utilitarians have long argued that the ideal code must include the familiar permissions and obligations, and the rights and freedoms, of common sense morality. Indeed, Hooker argues that 'the best argument for rule consequentialism is that it does a better job than its rivals of matching and tying together our moral convictions' (Hooker, 2000, p. 101). Human nature is not infinitely plastic. Any plausible code will include many familiar moral dispositions and distinctions such as honesty, generosity, promise-keeping, courage, murder-aversion, and so on. People who internalise the ideal code will not walk callously past children drowning in ponds, take pleasure in the sufferings of others, or reject the basic goods of human life.

One familiar objection is that utilitarianism is *unreasonably demanding* because it requires agents to always and everywhere treat their own interests on a par with the interests of everyone else (Hooker, 2000, pp. 159–74; Mulgan, 2001a). Derek Parfit argues that the general question of moral demandingness 'may be the most important moral question that most rich people face' (Parfit, 2011, vol. 1, p. 501). Hooker argues that while act utilitarianism cannot avoid extreme demands, rule utilitarianism can. This obviously requires a solution to the collapse objection. If rule utilitarianism does deliver the same results as act utilitarianism, then the two theories will obviously be equally demanding. If act utilitarianism is unreasonably demanding, then so is rule utilitarianism.

To avoid partial compliance absurdities, collapse into act utilitarianism, counter-intuitive results, and over-demandingness, rule utilitarians seek a middle ground between overly simplistic rules and infinitely complex ones. Many contemporary formulations of rule utilitarianism are driven by the need to differentiate the theory from act utilitarianism.

One solution is to examine the role of moral rules in human life. Human beings are not automata blindly complying with externally described patterns of behaviour. We are moral agents who seek to understand, accept, and follow moral rules. Hooker argues that rule utilitarians should ask what would happen if a given set of rules was *accepted* or *internalised* by everyone, where accepting a set of rules involves 'not just the disposition to comply with these rules, . . .

[but] also the disposition to encourage others to comply with them, dispositions to form favourable attitudes toward others who comply with them, dispositions to feel guilt or shame when one breaks them and to condemn and resent others' breaking them, all of which dispositions and attitudes being supported by the belief that they are justified' (Hooker, 2000, p. 76). He argues that the consequences of the *acceptance* of a rule within a population are not identical to the consequences of widespread compliance with that rule. Some people might accept a rule even though they do not always comply with it, while others might comply perfectly with a rule they do not accept. For instance, many people accept, on some level, more demanding principles regarding donations to charity than they can bring themselves to fully comply with, while social or legal sanctions often produce compliance without genuine acceptance.

More generally, all rule utilitarians argue that familiar facts about human psychology place limits on the complexity, demandingness, impartiality, or counter-intuitiveness of the ideal code. Some logically possible sets of rules are too intricate for anyone to understand, remember, or apply at all, while others would not produce good results even if we honestly tried to follow them. For instance, rule utilitarians ask us to imagine what a world where fallible partial human beings tried to follow act utilitarianism would really be like. They argue that, by purely utilitarian standards, act utilitarianism is not an ideal code of rules.

Parfit and Hooker thus respond to contrasting objections to act utilitarianism. Parfit worries that act utilitarianism is insufficiently demanding – in the sense that, by ignoring collective effects, it allows individuals to do things that ought to be forbidden. By contrast, Hooker worries that, in other cases, act utilitarianism is too demanding.

2.2.3 Introducing Ideal Outlook Utilitarianism

In my own recent work, I build on Hooker's rule utilitarianism to introduce a new collective utilitarianism whose central ethical question is: what moral outlook should we teach the next generation? (Mulgan, 2015b, 2017, 2018c.) This new theory honours utilitarianism's past and provides the flexibility to adapt to the full range of credible futures.

I dub my theory *Ideal Outlook Utilitarianism*. It begins by *directly collectively* evaluating moral outlooks, seeking the outlook that we should teach and encourage. But the resulting ideal outlook can play a variety of other roles. Once we identify it, we can use the ideal outlook for *indirect* evaluations. Individuals or groups could use the ideal outlook to guide their present deliberations about how to act.

Ideal outlook utilitarianism departs from Hooker's RU in two key ways. The first is largely terminological. Although 'rule utilitarianism' is the accepted name for a broad class of indirect collective utilitarian theories, I find talk of 'rules' and 'codes' distracting and potentially misleading. Talking instead of moral *outlooks* leaves open whether the utilitarian ideal is a code of rules, a set of dispositions, a package of virtues, a set of priorities, a general moral outlook, or (as seems most likely) some combination of these.

My second departure from traditional rule utilitarianism is more substantial, although it builds on Hooker's own theory. Rule utilitarianism standardly asks what would happen if we *ourselves* internalised, accepted, or followed any given moral code or outlook. Hooker asks us to imagine a code being internalised by a *new generation*. I ask instead what would happen if we (the present generation) attempted to *teach* a given outlook to the next generation. The *ideal* outlook is the best one for us to teach to them – not necessarily the best one for us to *follow*. Like Hooker, I set aside the cost of changing existing moral beliefs while factoring in the cost of (for instance) internalising a very demanding ethic. Unlike Hooker, I focus on our teaching of a moral outlook – highlighting the fact that before it can be internalised by one group, a moral outlook must actually be taught by another group.

However, ideal outlook utilitarianism is closer to Hooker's RU than it initially appears. 'Teaching' is not limited to explicit preaching about ethics. It also includes implicit lessons, role-modelling, story-telling, exemplification, and any other present behaviour that impacts on the moral outlook of those who are influenced by us. (The 'we' who teach thus includes any present person who could influence the moral outlook of people in that next generation.) Furthermore, the 'next generation' is an abstraction. Human beings are not bumble bees, arriving neatly packaged into discrete generations. The next generation is simply everyone directly influenced by our teaching.

Ideal outlook utilitarianism nonetheless has two distinctive features. First, it focuses primarily on the impact of our actions *on other people's moral outlook* (thus setting aside all other consequences), and second, it considers only people we directly influence – those we teach, as opposed to (say) people living in the distant future whose moral outlook may be influenced by our actions in many indirect ways.[6]

---

[6] While ideal outlook utilitarianism focuses *primarily* on our impact on the moral outlook of those we teach, impacts on other people cannot be completely ignored. Later impacts might matter in two possible cases. (1) As I discuss below, impacts on later generations – the descendants of the next generation whom we teach directly – are definitely included in any ideal outlook utilitarian calculation. (I am grateful to Dale Miller for pressing me on this point.) (2) If teaching a particular outlook to the next generation would be very costly *for us*, then this could, in principle, count against that outlook, even if its impact on future people would be optimal. (The cost to us might arise because (a) we could only teach that outlook effectively by internalising it and (b) such internalisation would severely disrupt our own lives.)

Ideal outlook utilitarianism always asks the same question: what can we teach now that will maximise well-being into the future? But this constant question receives different answers across the generations. What best promotes well-being in our generation may be neither what would have been best in the past nor what will be best in the future. Ideal outlook utilitarianism begins with a simple question and then allows complexity to emerge empirically, because the answer to that simple question depends on facts about human nature and about our ability to teach or learn moral outlooks. Ideal outlook utilitarianism's central question is timeless in its formulation but context-specific in its application.

I argue that ideal outlook utilitarianism has several advantages over its rivals in the recent utilitarian literature. First, ideal outlook utilitarianism captures a perennially attractive picture of morality as a collective human enterprise passed on from one generation to the next. Second, ideal outlook utilitarianism is closer to the spirit of the classical utilitarians, especially Jeremy Bentham and J. S. Mill. They too began with simple moral principles and allowed complexity to emerge empirically in response to our evolving knowledge of human nature and the human situation.

Third, ideal outlook utilitarianism's central empirical question is of independent interest, especially to moral educators. Other varieties of collective utilitarianism often ask questions that could never relate to any possible practical situation. (No one is ever in a position to choose whether or not everyone everywhere will follow some moral code.) By contrast, ideal outlook utilitarianism's question is practical. Indeed, if we interpret 'moral teaching' broadly, then that question is inescapable. We *will* teach the next generation *some* moral outlook. Ideal outlook utilitarianism asks what we *should* teach. Even if we don't use the ideal outlook to judge individual actions, we surely want to know which moral outlook it would be best to teach. Moral philosophers, moral educators, and others who observe that moral outlooks have changed in the past all ask how those outlooks might change in the future. And this prompts the further question: how *should* moral outlooks change? If we could get the next generation to follow, adopt, or internalise any moral outlook, which outlook should it be? If our job is to influence the next generation's moral outlook and we are at all sympathetic to utilitarianism, then the search for the ideal outlook obviously matters.

Fourth, I argue elsewhere that ideal outlook utilitarianism solves some puzzles that plague Hooker's RU (Mulgan, 2006, pp. 130–60). In particular, it neatly bypasses debates about what percentage of the ideal population should be assumed to have internalised the ideal outlook and to what extent (Hooker, 2000, pp. 80–5; Ridge, 2006; Hooker, 2008; Smith, 2010). As we saw earlier, if they want their ideal code of rules to cope with other people's wrongdoing, then rule utilitarians cannot idealise to *perfect* compliance. But any *specific* level of partial compliance seems ad hoc. Ideal outlook utilitarianism provides a simple solution. Instead of being stipulated ad hoc in advance, different degrees of internalisation reflect the relative difficulty of *teaching* different moral outlooks in different circumstances. The (expected) value of teaching an outlook may diverge from the (expected) value of internalising it, because some outlooks are easier to get other people to internalise. For instance, suppose (very artificially) that we face a choice between two moral outlooks: *demanding* and *moderate*. If someone internalises the demanding outlook, they will produce more future well-being than if they had internalised the moderate outlook. However, the demanding outlook is harder to teach. If we try to teach the demanding outlook, we will be less successful than if we try to teach the moderate outlook instead: fewer people in the next generation will internalise and obey the outlook that we teach them. Ideal outlook utilitarianism neatly balances these competing factors. We don't just ask how much good would result from successful internalisation. Nor do we focus exclusively on whether our teaching will be successful. Instead, we ask how much good would be produced *overall* if we tried to teach each competing outlook.

Finally, the best argument for ideal outlook utilitarianism is that it represents the most compelling utilitarian response to the challenges of future ethics. We need a utilitarian question that counts distant future people equally without asking us to imagine or imitate their moral thinking, and one that also allows for moral change. My new ideal outlook utilitarianism fits the bill perfectly. It focuses directly on the next generation and only indirectly on the distant future. Ideal outlook utilitarianism does not seek the outlook that would maximise well-being if it were followed by all subsequent generations. It asks only what we should teach *to the next generation.* On the other hand, the moral outlooks of later generations will enter our utilitarian calculations, because they are important consequences of our initial teaching.[7]

A central debate within utilitarianism is when we should idealise and when we should be realistic. For instance, act utilitarians idealise only *this individual agent's* actions – and keep everyone else's behaviour fixed. At the other extreme, some rule utilitarians implicitly idealise the behaviour of all moral agents – both present and future. Ideal outlook utilitarianism takes the middle

---

[7] This enables ideal outlook utilitarianism to avoid a new demandingness objection. What if a very demanding outlook would produce very significant benefits over many future generations? Won't those benefits outweigh a very high one-off cost in the first generation? Ideal outlook utilitarians reply that the costs of internalising a very demanding outlook will cascade down the generations – because the next generation will teach their own moral outlook to their successors. (I am grateful to an anonymous reviewer for pressing me on this point.)

ground. It idealises only the behaviour of the present generation. It asks what it would be best for us to teach, but it does not project this imaginary utilitarian thought experiment into the future. Ideal outlook utilitarianism does not ask what outlook it would be best for the next generation to teach the third generation. It asks instead what would actually happen if we teach this outlook to the next generation. This includes also asking what outlook the next generation will *actually* teach – and what effects their teaching will have on later generations. After all, this is how moral education works. We teach the next generation. We cannot teach distant future people.

Like Hooker's RU, ideal outlook utilitarianism limits the potential alien-ness of the ideal outlook, because that outlook must be taught by current human beings to a new generation of humans. Trying to teach a outlook that is too demanding or alien to human nature would not have good consequences! However, ideal outlook utilitarianism also departs from common sense morality in some important ways and offers guidance where common sense morality is silent or confused. In particular, ideal outlook utilitarianism will depart from current moral practice in at least four cases. (1) Sometimes, our current moral practice falls short of our own current common sense morality. We don't act as well as we already know that we should. In these cases, ideal outlook utilitarianism sides with our better natures. (2) Current common sense morality is often unclear or inconsistent. Resolving inconsistencies is clearly a good idea from a utilitarian perspective, and ideal outlook utilitarianism tries to resolve them. (3) Changing circumstances bring out new or underappreciated inconsistencies or anomalies in current common sense morality. For instance, many utilitarians argue that our ability to affect people on the other side of the world may force us to re-examine our ideas about our obligations to distant strangers. And, as we saw earlier, Parfit argued that modern life makes it imperative that we abandon our exclusive focus on the direct effects of individual acts. As a form of *collective* utilitarianism, ideal outlook utilitarianism follows Parfit here. (4) Finally, current common sense morality is not adequate to the new ethical challenges posed by many credible possible futures. Any plausible utilitarian future ethic must therefore go beyond current common sense morality to make sense of those futures. In particular, as I argue in section 2.3, the ideal moral outlook for a *broken* future diverges sharply from our current moral common sense. However, I regard these divergences as an objection to common sense morality, not as a problem for ideal outlook utilitarianism. Our considered moral judgements have evolved to fit our affluent world. We cannot reasonably expect them to be (even) prima facie reliable when we contemplate a broken future.

This is only a sketch of ideal outlook utilitarianism. Two main topics require further exploration. The first is that many details remain unresolved. As one reader notes, 'the outcomes of teaching an outlook crucially depend on *who* does it, to *whom* it is taught, and *how* it is taught'. I have only provided very general answers to these questions. I imagine everyone currently alive using the best available standard human ways to teach moral lessons to those who will come after us. The boundaries between acceptable teaching and unacceptable manipulation are vague. We presumably want to rule out invasive neurosurgery that re-programmes the next generation's brain patterns so that they can follow inhumanly intricate or demanding rules. (What useful moral guidance could we gain from that?) On the other hand, we presumably want to allow for improvements in schooling or diet that predictably enhance moral performance. Ideal outlook utilitarianism leaves many hostages to empirical fortune: much depends on how plastic and flexible human moral learning actually is. But this uncertainty is in keeping with the traditional utilitarian commitment to empiricism.

A second topic for future exploration is the connection between ideal moral teaching and other moral evaluations. Ideal outlook utilitarianism offers a direct evaluation of *our moral teaching*. Does it also provide *indirect* evaluations of *right action*? This new theory directly answers a new question. Does it also provide new answers to old questions? In particular, suppose we identify the best outlook for us to teach the next generation. Should we ourselves now follow that outlook? Ideal outlook utilitarianism is most interesting – but also most controversial – when it argues that we should.[8] Like Hooker's RU, ideal outlook utilitarianism seeks a middle ground between two extremes. On the one hand, asking us to follow the outlook that maximises value *if everyone follows it* is unreasonably demanding – because it ignores the limitations on our human ability to internalise or learn a moral code. On the other hand, asking us to

---

[8] Another theoretical option is that we should be guided by the moral outlook that it *would have been best for the previous generation to have taught to us*, rather than the moral outlook that it would be best for us to teach to the next generation. I set this complication aside in the text, because these outlooks are likely to be identical or at least very similar. So long as conditions do not change *too* rapidly from one generation to the next, the best outlook for us to teach *is* the best one for us to have been taught. However, the two outlooks could come apart. If times are changing very rapidly, and if the next generation's challenges will be very different from our own, then the best outlook for us to teach may not be the one that it would have been best for our parents to teach to us. In such a case, ideal outlook utilitarians will need to decide which outlook they should follow. (I am grateful to Dale Miller for pressing me on this point.)

One striking illustration of the possibility of rapid intergenerational change arises at the very end of human history. Suppose we discover that some unpreventable catastrophe will wipe out humanity in a hundred years. The members of the present generation ask what they should teach the next generation – knowing that the latter will be the last in human history. These two generations face quite different moral challenges, and the best outlook to teach the penultimate generation may diverge sharply from the outlook they should teach to the very last humans. In particular, the two generations will need very different attitudes to procreation! (I explore the moral challenges of human extinction in section 4.6 and at greater length in Mulgan, 2018d, 2019, and forthcoming a.)

follow the 'best' (in utilitarian terms) outlook that *we* could internalise is too undemanding – because it makes unnecessary concessions to our existing (very suboptimal) moral dispositions. We should strive instead to follow the best outlook that one group of human adults *could* teach to another. And that is the ideal moral outlook.

A more modest alternative theory would combine our ideal outlook account of moral teaching with direct or indirect evaluations drawn from other utilitarian theories. In this section, I have presented three collective departures from act utilitarianism. Each could be explored on its own. However, Parfit's collective evaluation of acts, Hooker's rule utilitarianism, and my own ideal outlook utilitarianism could also be incorporated into a *pluralist* utilitarian ethic, where a range of different foci are each evaluated directly (cf. Driver, 2014). Such pluralism is arguably closer to the spirit of the classical utilitarians. For instance, a utilitarian moral agent might find themselves trying to balance potentially very demanding direct evaluations of their own individual acts and their contribution to collective patterns of behaviour with the less radical deliverances of the rule utilitarian ideal code or some general obligation to teach the next generation the best possible moral outlook. There is no a priori reason to expect the best utilitarian ethic to be tidy!

This completes our direct exploration of collective and indirect utilitarianism. Some aspects of the utilitarian future ethic developed in the rest of this Element are independent of these debates – they can fit into any utilitarian theory, whether it is direct or indirect, individual or collective. But the introduction of collectivism and indirect evaluation also makes available new possibilities for utilitarian future ethics.

2.3 Why Utilitarianism Must Accommodate Broken Futures

Collective utilitarianism presents itself as a moderate, liberal, intuitively plausible alternative to individual act utilitarianism. One immediate challenge is whether this defence is still credible once we take account of the full range of credible futures. In particular, can any moderate liberal utilitarianism survive the transition to a broken future?

All collective utilitarians share the general consequentialist commitment to temporal impartiality. We seek the moral outlook that best promotes individual welfare into the distant future. But an outlook designed to cope with extreme future scarcity may place very significant demands on the next generation – and (by extension) on us. If we judge *our own moral obligations* by asking what future people living in a broken future would feel free to do, we may find ourselves obliged to make great sacrifices.

We must separate two questions. (1) What is the best moral outlook for us to bequeath to future people who might be living in a broken world? (2) Insofar as the best utilitarian ethic for a broken future differs from our present ethics, should we embrace it?

I begin by exploring utilitarianism *within* the broken future. Suppose we know that our descendants *will* inhabit a broken future. What moral outlook should we pass down? Will future people be best served by a liberal utilitarian moral outlook? In particular, how might that ideal outlook differ from either (a) our current common sense morality or (b) the moral outlook that it *would* have been best to pass down if we were instead confident that our descendants would inherit an unbroken world?

In my own recent work, I argue that current ethical thinking must be re-imagined in many ways for a broken future. While some specific impacts of the broken world are predictable, others are more surprising.[9] One general lesson is that the ethical outlook of a broken future society may be very austere (Mulgan, 2011, 2015b, 2017). Scarcity of material resources (especially water) and an unpredictable climate will create periodic population bottlenecks where not everyone can survive. (This is what the loss of Rawlsian favourable conditions *means*.) When *nothing* (not even bare survival) can be guaranteed to everyone, rights must be either abandoned or radically re-invented. Social survival in a broken world may require restrictions on personal liberty on a scale that people have only previously accepted in times of war or other temporary crisis. Private land and individual labour might be requisitioned to grow food, the use of fossil fuels for private purposes might be severely curtailed, and individual lifestyle choices – especially reproductive decisions – might be regulated and constrained much more than we would currently accept. Our affluent liberal ethics, designed for a world of enduring favourable conditions and emphasising individual *rights*, is thus particularly *ill-suited* to a broken world. This is why the broken future is so ethically unsettling.

In *Ethics for a Broken World*, I introduce the metaphor of a survival lottery. I argue that any broken world *society* must find a way to manage extreme scarcity. It must therefore institute some *survival lottery*: some bureaucratic procedure that determines who lives and who dies. And no broken world society

---

[9] For instance, I argue elsewhere that the following philosophical ideas must all be re-imagined to fit a broken world: versions of naturalistic meta-ethics that identify moral facts with the end-points of processes of empirical moral inquiry that may turn out to be inextricably linked to an unsustainable way of life (Jackson, 1999; Mulgan, 2015b), the many strands of contemporary moral philosophy built on intuitions that are very closely tied to our affluent present (Singer, 1972; Thomson, 1976; Mulgan, 2015d), and theories of rights and distributive justice that implicitly presume a world where the central elements of a worthwhile life can be guaranteed to everyone (Mulgan, 2011, pp. 18–68; 2018a).

will endure unless most citizens regard its actual survival lottery as (at least reasonably) just. A central concern of broken world ethics is thus to design a *just* survival lottery.

'Survival lottery' is a term of art. It may not involve any *actual* lottery. For instance, a *libertarian* survival lottery might simply consist of a collective decision to allow the 'natural' distribution of survival chances to remain uncorrected. But broken world *utilitarians* are extremely unlikely to embrace this libertarian extreme. Instead, they will seek a fair and efficient re-distribution of the burdens imposed by scarce resources and a chaotic climate. A central question here, as so often for utilitarians, is how we should balance the competing demands of fairness and efficiency.

All broken world ethicists must be prepared to countenance trade-offs between lives and to sacrifice present basic needs to preserve or enhance their society's capacity to meet future basic needs. In a world of declining or fluctuating resources, a sustainable survival lottery cannot always privilege the present over the future. *Any* adequate broken world moral outlook must therefore include a willingness to *contemplate* survival lotteries, to ask which possible survival lotteries are *more* just, and to endorse an existing survival lottery if (but only if) it is reasonably just. The transition to a broken future thus supports utilitarianism over its non-utilitarian rivals. Utilitarianism adapts more readily to changing circumstances, because all utilitarian commitments are already contingent and revisable. Utilitarianism is often attacked for its willingness to think the unthinkable. The twentieth-century English philosopher Elizabeth Anscombe went so far as to describe utilitarian thinking as the product of a corrupt mind (Anscombe, 1957, pp. 16–17). In a broken world, where the unthinkable must be thought, this willingness becomes not a vice but a necessary virtue.

The transition to a broken future would also undermine many non-utilitarian claims about the importance of rights. Most natural rights theorists concede that *present* property rights are only justified if they benefit (or at least do not harm) *future* people. (For instance, many libertarians enshrine this commitment in Lockean provisos, where my acquisition of property is only legitimate if I leave 'enough and as good' for others, and those 'others' include future people.) In our affluent world, these future-directed constraints remain in the background, because philosophers routinely take it for granted that future people will be better off than present people. In a broken future, by contrast, the demand that we leave future people no worse off would move centre-stage. This development will have both practical and theoretical consequences. Practically, future broken world philosophers will deny that *our* property rights were *ever* legitimate, because our exercise of those rights has left our descendants worse off due to climate change.[10] They will therefore deny that individuals or groups in their broken world could possibly have inherited any property rights from our affluent world. At a theoretical level, future philosophers will also reject natural rights theories that present rights as absolute side-constraints. They will instead be much more sympathetic to forward-looking utilitarian accounts where rights are justified by future benefits and constrained by changing circumstances. Without individual rights, non-utilitarianism loses much of its ethical distinctiveness.

As well as supporting utilitarianism, the transition to a broken future also transforms it.[11] Utilitarianism will be even more demanding in the broken world than it is today. All broken world inhabitants are much more willing than ourselves to make sacrifices for the common good. (Evidence from earlier eras when people often lived in less abundant circumstances strongly suggests that greater self-sacrifice is *possible*. And a broken world *society* – especially one whose foundations are not xenophobic or otherwise ethically unacceptable – is impossible without it.) Given their own grim history, future utilitarians will also take their own intergenerational obligations much more seriously than we do, as well as placing greater importance on collective and intergenerational projects.

Within utilitarianism, broken world ethics will favour collectivism over individualism. In a broken world, collective survival demands social co-operation on an unprecedented scale. Broken world thinkers will attach much greater significance to the ability to recognise, respect, and safeguard the long-term collective interests of human beings. (Broken world philosophers will not make Parfit's mistakes in moral mathematics.) Nurturing and developing this ability will be the central task of moral education and public institutions.

In addition, familiar liberal utilitarian arguments (inspired by J. S. Mill) about the desirability of broad participation in the design of political institutions are *especially* compelling in a broken world (Mulgan, 2011, pp. 133–47). The broken world ideal outlook will definitely not favour unthinking acceptance of the status quo.

These reflections on life in a possible broken future are sobering. Thinking about the challenges our descendants might face hopefully prompts us to take our own intergenerational obligations more seriously. But ideal outlook utilitarianism goes further – as will most other collective utilitarians. Predictions

---

[10] The scope of 'our' here includes most readers of this Element – and certainly anyone over the age of fifty.

[11] The rest of this section draws freely on my earlier work. It also extends my previous discussions of broken world ethics by highlighting the connections between our predictions of future utilitarian thinking and our present utilitarian obligations.

about the moral outlook of future people are intertwined with judgements about how they (and we) should act. We expect that future utilitarians – living in a broken world – *will* adopt a more demanding, self-abnegating, and collective morality, in part because we recognise that they *should*. And our judgements about what *they* should do also influence our judgements about *our own* obligations.

The moral outlook that it would be best for us to bequeath also determines *how we should act now*. Ideal outlook utilitarianism consciously links *present obligations* to *future ethics*. This is not an arbitrary or ad hoc manoeuvre. It has a principled justification. Utilitarians embrace temporal impartiality. Future people's welfare matters as much as our own. We cannot reasonably insist on privileges and permissions that they cannot enjoy. If our descendants might face the harsh choices of a broken future, then perhaps we should too. Rule utilitarianism and ideal outlook utilitarianism are both self-consciously forward-looking theories: assuming *that our most important moral focus is the future*, they invite us to embrace their demanding future ethic as our own contemporary moral ideal.

The ideal moral outlook for a broken world does not mirror what we now think morality demands of us. However, as moral philosophers, we should ask not what we currently believe, but what we *would* believe if we reflected in the light of all the morally relevant facts. The discovery that our world faces (or might face) a broken future *is* a morally relevant fact that *should* impact on our rights, permissions, and obligations. The very factors that lead ideal outlook or rule utilitarians to offer different verdicts in a broken world should also lead *us*, as reflective moral thinkers, to change our moral beliefs.

Utilitarian future ethics issues the following sobering challenges: can we reasonably insist that morality demand *less* of affluent people facing a broken future than it does of people already living in a broken world? Or that it demand less of us than we have reason to believe that future people will *think* it demanded of us? How could we justify such discrepancies *to future people in a broken world*?

By keeping the inhabitants of the broken future in mind and asking how our collective behaviour affects their well-being, we bring our considered moral judgements into line with theirs. Our ideal moral outlook will be aligned with our considered moral judgements, because both have been radically transformed. And because the two transformations respond to the same underlying facts about life in the broken futures, there is good reason to expect them to move in tandem. The ideal outlook for us to bequeath to a broken future will fit our *considered* judgements of what morality demands – both in that future and in our affluent present – even if it doesn't fit our *current* ethical judgements.

3 Well-Being and Possible Futures

3.1 What Is Well-Being?

In this section, I outline some central debates about the content and scope of well-being. Later sections ask how reflection on possible futures and the adoption of a collective perspective might transform or inform those debates.

Many introductions to utilitarianism begin with individual well-being. My reason for not doing so is that adopting an indirect collective approach enables us to distinguish several different roles that any particular story about well-being (or any other aspect of value) can play in our overall utilitarian theory. It can be offered as an account of (1) the *foundational* values that we use to select our ideal code of rules or moral outlook, (2) the values that would be adopted by someone who had *internalised* that code or outlook, (3) the values *we* should use when we apply that code or outlook in our own situation, (4) the values that we would use in Parfit-style direct collective evaluations of our own acts, or (5) the values that an individual agent should use to directly evaluate their own actions. In principle, a single utilitarian theory might deploy different values in each of these roles. I believe that distinguishing these roles can help us to make progress on a range of seemingly intractable debates within utilitarian value theory.

Utilitarians seek to promote well-being. But the nature of human well-being is a site of perennial philosophical controversy. We are unsure what makes life worth living. Parfit conveniently contrasts three positions: *hedonism* says that well-being is pleasure and the absence of pain; *preference theory* says that well-being is getting what you want; and the *objective list theory* offers a list of things that are good in themselves irrespective of the agent's attitude to them, such as knowledge, achievement, friendship, and so on (Parfit, 1984, pp. 3–4, 493–502; Fletcher, 2013; Bradley, 2014; Crisp, 2015). Objectivists argue that neither hedonism nor preference theory is satisfactory. Some pleasures are good, some are bad, others are neutral. Some preferences improve your life, while others do not. Consider a child who wants to play in the sand rather than go to school. Clearly, we make their life go better if we send them to school. The challenge is to explain *why*. Education doesn't simply help people to satisfy their existing preferences. It also teaches them what to desire and which pleasures to seek. It is important to satisfy people's desires only *because* what they value is independently worthwhile. The objects are not valuable because they are desired – they are desired because they are valuable.

A theory of well-being is an account of what is *intrinsically* valuable to the person themselves, as opposed to a list of things that are *instrumentally* valuable. However, the standard distinction between intrinsic and instrumental value can be confusing. I prefer a tripartite distinction (adapted from debates in environmental philosophy) where instrumental value is contrasted with both *inherent* value and *independent* value. A thing's inherent value is its non-instrumental value to me, while its independent value is the value it has in its own right independent of any connection to any agent. In the present context, the achievement of something that has independent value may be inherently valuable to me.

Each theory comes in many variations, and further specification often blurs the boundaries between Parfit's three categories. (For further debate, see, e.g., Griffin, 1986; Crisp, 2006; Dorsey, 2012; Woodard, 2013; Bradley, 2014; Heathwood, 2014.[12]) Most objectivists include pleasure (and the absence of pain) as one primary list item. (Indeed, we could interpret hedonism itself as an objective theory whose list has only one item.) While preference satisfaction is not always explicitly listed, most lists include some closely related item such as freedom, choice, autonomy, or self-determination. And some objectivists supplement their entire list with enjoyment, knowledge, or choice requirements – arguing that independently valuable items such as achievement and knowledge only enhance an individual's well-being if (1) they give the individual pleasure, and/or (2) the individual is aware of them, and/or (3) they are freely chosen or consciously endorsed.

From the other direction, many hedonists distinguish different *kinds* of pleasure. This suggestion goes back to J. S. Mill's infamous distinction between 'higher' and 'lower' pleasures. Anxious to combine Benthamite hedonism with the view that some activities are intrinsically more worthwhile than others, Mill introduced 'competent judges' who are familiar with both activities and discern which pleasure is 'more desirable' (Mill, 1963, vol. 10, pp. 211–13). Similarly, many actual preferences are frivolous, counter-productive, pointless, noxious, or unrelated to one's own welfare. Commonly discussed counter-examples include: hypothetical desires to spend one's life eating mud or counting blades of grass; (sadly not hypothetical) desires to inflict pain, suffering, or humiliation on others; and non-self-regarding desires such as the hope that there is life elsewhere in the universe. More 'sophisticated' contemporary preference theorists therefore introduce some element of idealisation. What makes your life go well is not the satisfaction of *all* your desires but only of those desires about

---

[12] Parfit's tripartite division is controversial for other reasons. Two common worries are (1) that Parfit elides the crucial distinction between what *is* good for us and what *makes* it good, and (2) that he obscures the distinction between subjective and objective accounts of well-being. For instance, suppose that a hedonist says that pleasure is good *because it is pleasant*. We could characterise this view as objective. But is it more natural to treat hedonism as subjective – because it grounds well-being in subjective feelings, whereas a genuinely objective theory would offer a non-subjective different account of *why* its chosen list items were inherently good (Woodard, 2013)?

your own life (sometimes called 'I-desires') that you would retain if you laundered your desires through some process of ideal deliberation or reflection. Finally, as a nod to hedonism, preference theorists often tie well-being not to the bare fact that one's preferences *are satisfied* but to the felt-and-acknowledged fact that they are fulfilled.

Another explanation for apparent disagreements is that different accounts of well-being may play different theoretical or practical roles. For instance, particularly in economics, a reliance on preference satisfaction is often most plausibly construed as a recognition that markets within a liberal society should respect individual tastes, rather than as a theory of what *constitutes* well-being.

However, I believe that Parfit's tripartite division is still useful. Each position has some non-negotiable commitments. For the hedonist, well-being is simply a matter of what goes on in your head. (What you don't experience isn't good for you.) For the preference theorist, your actual preferences remain the final arbiters of your well-being. (What you don't desire isn't good for you.) For the objectivist, a life full of pleasure, satisfaction, or fulfilment could still be lacking something essential for a truly worthwhile human life. Borrowing the terminology of ideal preference theory, objectivists insist that 'ideal deliberation' must also include the ability to correctly identify the *independent* value of competing *objects* of desire. Furthermore, objectivists will argue that reflection on possible futures teaches us that something vital is missing if future people *lack* certain specific good desires – even if all their actual desires are both good and satisfied. (For instance, a desired and enjoyed connection to non-human nature could be essential for a flourishing human life, even if someone who has never imagined such a desire had no idea what they were missing.)

In sections 3.3, 3.4, and 3.5, we ask how contemporary debates about the content of well-being might be transformed in a range of possible futures – especially broken, virtual, and digital futures. We first explore another central utilitarian question: whose well-being counts?

3.2 Utilitarianism and Non-human Nature

Thus far, we have focused on the well-being of humans. But utilitarians have always been interested in the moral significance of non-human animals – and especially their suffering. Indeed, many contemporary utilitarians regard *non-speciesism* as an essential and appealing feature of the utilitarian moral outlook. We must define our circle of moral concern by citing the *general* properties of individuals, not their membership of the human species. For Bentham, what matters is whether an individual can suffer (Bentham, 1996, chapter 17). For Mill, while higher pleasures are more important than lower pleasures, this would only (at most) contingently give lower priority to the pleasures of non-human animals. Any non-human animal that could enjoy higher pleasures would have the same moral status as an equivalently capable human. For the preference theorist, everything turns on whether or not non-human animals can be truly said to have preferences or desires. At the very least, most sentient animals do seem to prefer to avoid agony! Some items on many objective lists – such as knowledge, achievement, or autonomy – may well be inaccessible to many non-human animals. However, the presence of pleasure (and especially the absence of pain) on most lists means that animals cannot be ignored.

Including non-human animals pushes utilitarianism in radical directions – regarding both our treatment of animals and our treatment of severely disabled humans. Utilitarians insist that we should treat non-human animals no worse than equally capable humans. While opponents suggest that this means we will mistreat some humans, utilitarians reply that, if we would not treat a human in a particular way, then we shouldn't treat non-human animals like that either. (See, especially, Singer, 1975, 2011.)

A striking feature of recent ethics is the rise of environmental philosophy. Environmental philosophers reject the anthropocentrism of traditional Western philosophy, arguing that non-human nature must be valued in its own right. Environmental philosophy offers four accounts of the moral significance of non-human nature. *Anthropocentrism* focuses on the ways that non-human nature matters to human beings. *Sentientism* argues that all sentient beings – whether human or not – matter. *Biocentrism* argues that all living beings – whether sentient or not – matter. Finally, for *ecocentrism*, the primary locus of value is the ecosystem as a whole. Individual living things (including human beings) matter only insofar as they contribute to thriving ecosystems. Environmental philosophy includes both consequentialist and non-consequentialist responses to these values, depending on whether the value of non-human nature is primarily to be promoted or respected.

Utilitarians are already committed to sentientism. Non-human nature is therefore clearly relevant to utilitarianism in several ways. First, in any plausible account of well-being, non-human nature has very great *instrumental* value for human beings. Without flourishing animals, plants, and ecosystems, we cannot survive. Second, non-human nature may have *inherent* value as a separate component of human well-being. For instance, some objective list theories regard a close connection to the non-human natural world as valuable in itself. Human lives go better (and perhaps can only go well) when they instantiate that value. Third, if non-human animals can suffer, then all utilitarians regard their welfare as *independently* valuable irrespective of its relation to humans.

What about the 'interests' or 'significance' of non-sentient non-human nature? Many environmental philosophers regard sentientism as unduly narrow. Biocentrism and ecocentrism call for expansions of our sphere of moral concern that are analogous to the expansion to include animal welfare. However, many utilitarians will argue that, whatever their merits, biocentrism and ecocentrism effectively abandon the central utilitarian concern for the flourishing of beings capable of experiencing pleasure and pain. Non-human animals matter if – *but only if* – they are sentient. Plants and ecosystems are clearly not sentient. Therefore, despite their enormous instrumental (and perhaps inherent) importance, they cannot possess any independent value.

Environmental philosophers who wish to include biocentric or ecocentric obligations or reasons could then defend a pluralist ethical theory that combines these with utilitarian reasons based on the well-being of humans and animals. If our biocentrism or ecocentrism takes a consequentialist form, then the former obligations or reasons could also be modelled on utilitarianism.

As we'll see in the rest of this section, future ethics introduces new conflicts between human and non-human interests, raises new questions about the value of non-human nature, and introduces new classes of beings whose well-being might matter – digital beings or extraterrestrials.

3.3 Well-Being and Broken Futures

Having introduced the main debates about the substance and scope of utilitarian concern for well-being, this rest of this section explores these familiar debates through the lens of three possible futures: broken, virtual, and digital. We can ask three questions about any possible future: how might debates about well-being change *in that future*? How *should* future utilitarians think about well-being? And what does reflection on that future teach *us* about well-being? I begin with the broken future.

While we cannot predict future debates about well-being in any detail, we can make some tentative predictions. We should not expect complete discontinuity. Broken world moral philosophers will still debate the relative merits of pleasure, preference, and objective value. But they will balance competing considerations differently. As I argued in section 2.3 above, relative to our affluent present, people immersed in a broken future will (1) attach more significance to collective or collaborative projects, (2) emphasise synergies between individual well-being and social utility, and (3) dismiss many things that we regard as essential components of a truly worthwhile human life as unnecessary and unattainable luxuries. And utilitarianism encourages these developments. Although it urges agents to improve things, utilitarianism also encourages future people to be content with their lot as far as possible – to focus on what is available in their reduced circumstances rather than striving for what is no longer attainable. The moral outlook that maximises well-being in a broken future – however well-being is defined or measured – will not retain our affluent priorities and obsessions.

Future people for whom the broken world is an unavoidable reality will inevitably adapt to it. And utilitarians will encourage this adaptation. Desires that can no longer be satisfied simply bring unhappiness. If we know that our descendants will definitely inhabit a broken future, then we should promote this adaptation – bequeathing them a moral outlook that doesn't pine after lost affluence. But this very adaptability is a double-edged sword. Suppose instead that we must choose between *creating* a broken future and bearing a significant cost ourselves to avert that future. Imagine an unscrupulous (or idealistic) preference theorist, employed perhaps by some corporation with a vested interest in the affluent status quo, defending the imposition of a broken future in the following terms:

> As utilitarians, we seek to maximise our descendants' well-being. Well-being is entirely a function of the satisfaction of actual preferences. (Anything else would be paternalistic!) We could, of course, sink vast sums into mitigating catastrophic climate change and other environmental degradation. But this would greatly reduce the satisfaction of *our own existing* preferences – not to mention those new preferences our ingenious marketing department is continually creating. For a fraction of the cost, at comparatively little inconvenience to ourselves, we could instead invest in the development of our patented PanglossPlus psychological adaptation system. This would ensure that, however restricted their natural, cultural, or environmental resources, our descendants will be perfectly happy with their lot. They will thank us for bequeathing a world so perfectly tuned to their own natural desires, and they would laugh incredulously at the very idea that anyone would regard such a utopian situation as broken or deficient. (Terms and conditions apply. Other dystopias are available.)

The prospect of a broken future thus exacerbates a perennial Achilles heel of preference theory – the threat of adaptive preferences. As I will now argue, this problem is most acute if we consider a future that is both broken *and virtual*.

3.4 Well-Being and Virtual Futures

Recall *our virtual future* where people have abandoned the real world altogether and spend their entire lives plugged into an experience machine that perfectly simulates any possible human experience. Such a virtual reality might emerge as the best option in a broken world. The natural environment is so polluted and so resource-poor that people have little choice but to dream away their lives with no direct contact to any reality outside the machine. This is not a sceptical scenario. Future people are fully aware that their reality is merely virtual. But this is all anyone has ever known, and they find it perfectly satisfactory. No one misses bird song, clean air, blue skies, or any of the other wonders their rapacious ancestors have destroyed.

The virtual world has many advocates, and some people are striving to make it a reality. Our first question, then, is whether the virtual world *is* undesirable. Should this future worry us? Should we try to avoid it? If individuals are the best judges of their own interests, then the virtual future is unobjectionable. All that matters is that people are content with their lot. But is this correct?

My virtual future is modelled on Robert Nozick's famous experience machine (Nozick, 1974, 42–5). Like many good thought experiments, it works by prising apart things that typically go together. When pleasure is entirely cut adrift from achievement, which matters more? Nozick's discussion is tantalisingly brief, and his dialectical purpose is unclear. However, one popular interpretation presents Nozick's thought experiment as a reductio ad absurdum of hedonism (Feldman, 2011). Nozick argues that it is a mistake to choose the experience machine. Experience is not the only thing that matters. We want to *do* things, not merely to have the illusion of doing them. And we need a connection to some reality that is deeper than the imagination of a video game designer.

Nozick's thought experiment is so powerful because many people share his reaction that something vital *is* lost if one spends one's entire life in a virtual world, however perfectly it replicates the real thing. And an *actual* virtual future would be even more worrying than Nozick's original tale. Nozick imagines each individual both (1) deciding for themselves whether to enter the machine and then (2) selecting their own experiences from a menu of possible fantasy scenarios. By contrast, if the escape to virtual reality is the only option in a broken future, then even if future people can choose some details of their virtual world, they cannot choose it *in preference to some desirable non-virtual alternative*. Future people may *prefer* their virtual world, but they have not *chosen* it. Anyone who thinks it is a mistake to enter the experience machine should find the imposition of a virtual future especially troubling.

Suppose we agree that a virtual future is both credible and undesirable. How would this affect our current ethical thinking? In the first place, reflection on the potential deficiencies of virtual futures reinforces the importance of our obligations to future people. We cannot blithely assume that new technology will enable future people to escape the broken world, because some technological 'solutions' are themselves undesirable. Rather than being a route to eternal happiness, virtual futures might leave future people worse off than present people in very important ways.

A credible virtual future also sheds new light on debates about the nature of well-being. By definition, life in any experience machine is phenomenologically indistinguishable from the 'real thing'. Hedonists must find the virtual world unobjectionable. If the imposition of a virtual future is objectionable, then there must be more to human flourishing than the quality of one's experiences. Therefore, hedonism is false.

Preference theory also cannot explain our unease about the imposition of a virtual future whose inhabitants are content with their lot. If we only look at individual preferences, we cannot see what is wrong with avoiding our obligations to future people simply by manipulating their psychology – or their environment – so that they never want the good things we destroy.

The virtual future thus supports *objectivism* about well-being, because only an objective account can capture both Nozick's worries about the experience machine and our worries about the virtual future. These reactions suggest that we regard a connection to the natural world as *inherently* valuable. It matters that people are connected to real values, not virtual ones. Even Peter Singer, the most prominent contemporary defender of preference utilitarianism, has recently acknowledged, on the basis of very similar examples, that we need a more objective account of well-being to make sense of our obligations to distant future people (Singer, 2011, p. 244).[13]

The virtual future nicely illustrates the philosophical significance of transforming imaginary thought experiments into possible realities. When Nozick first presented it in 1974, the experience machine was science fiction. In 2019, the virtual world is one credible future. Something like this could well happen. Even if we discount the hype surrounding all new technologies, no one can be confident that genuine virtual reality will not emerge. The virtual world may not be our immediate future. Indeed, it may never happen. (Some future catastrophe might prevent the necessary technology from ever emerging.) But it is one medium-term possibility. (And even if perfect virtual reality remains forever elusive, milder trade-offs between the virtual and the real are already here.)

This credibility greatly strengthens the objectivist critique of hedonism and preference theory. In debates over well-being, as in many other philosophical topics, every theory stumbles over some ingenious imaginary case. Defenders of hedonism or preference theory could argue that their inability to capture our

---

[13] However, Singer does not endorse objective list theory. Instead, his more objective account of well-being is hedonist. As well as intuitive considerations relating to future people, Singer's rejection of preference theory is also associated with his rejection of Hare's prescriptivist meta-ethic in favour of Parfit's more objective moral realism. (I am grateful to an anonymous reviewer for pressing me to clarify these points.)

intuitions about Nozick's experience machine is not a decisive objection, because no theory captures *all* our intuitions.

We cannot insist that a theory of well-being must perfectly fit all our intuitions about imaginary cases. But we can reasonably require moral philosophy to provide useful guidance about important actual decisions. An acceptable theory of well-being must help us to think clearly about our obligations regarding credible futures, especially when our present choices might harm future people.

Singer's own conversion is instructive here. As a practical ethicist, Singer focuses on first-order moral issues, such as abortion, our treatment of animals, or our obligations to the distant poor. His shift away from preference utilitarianism is driven by the failure of his own attempts to apply the theory to the newly urgent practical questions posed by climate change. The practical ethicist can sidestep the experience machine but not the virtual future.

The virtual future creates challenges for all ethical theories. But these challenges are especially significant for utilitarians because of the central importance they place on well-being. If utilitarians object to the virtual future, they *must* appeal to the inherent value of real-world connections *as a component of individual human well-being.*

Virtual futures also illuminate another site of perennial ethical disagreement. Like many non-human animals, human beings are social creatures. Everyone agrees that a flourishing human life must involve good relationships with others. But are these interpersonal relations inherently valuable or merely instrumentally useful? (E.g., Finnis, 1980, pp. 88, 141–4; Griffin, 1986, pp. 64–8.) In real life, this question may never arise, because the instrumental value of interpersonal relations includes the pleasure we derive from them – and that pleasure couldn't actually have any other source. Instead, philosophers rely on imaginary cases where a person's 'friends' are merely actors playing a part. (*The Truman Show* is an extreme case of this.) Suppose the person never discovers the deceit. That person's experiences are exactly as they would be if their friends were genuine. Does their life go worse than someone with identical experiences who does have genuine friends? Hedonists must say no. Preference theorists and objectivists can disagree. What the person experiences is not actually the satisfaction of their preferences or the inherent good of friendship. Therefore, their experiences don't have the value that the person thinks they have.

The contrast between two possible virtual futures offers another striking test case. In an *interpersonal* virtual future, different flesh-and-blood people inhabit the same shared virtual world, while in a *solipsist* virtual future, each person is alone in their own private virtual world. If friendship is only a means to enjoyment, then a solipsist experience machine that simulates *the experience of having friends* is perfectly adequate. But many people would regard this as a very poor substitute for *real* friendship. Stories such as *The Matrix* and *The Truman Show* are so unsettling precisely *because* we regard friendship as an end in itself, not merely an in-principle-replaceable means. But how could hedonists object to a solipsist virtual future? And how could preference theorists object if future solipsists are content to inhabit their own virtual worlds?

A closely related issue is the place of non-human animals in the virtual future. Should hedonists campaign for each sentient animal to be given its own experience machine? (If so, who will choose and programme its experiences?) And should humans and animals in virtual worlds be able to experience real connections with (other) animals – or would virtual replacement pets be sufficient? In a broken future, where hard choices have to be made, will any resources at all be devoted to the welfare of non-human animals once humans have escaped into virtual worlds? Debates about the inherent and independent value of non-human nature thus come to the fore in virtual futures – and in any non-virtual present where virtual futures are credible.

Virtual futures thus introduce a host of new and challenging ethical questions. A perennial theme of science fiction is that adapting to life in a virtual environment would be very unsettling. It is not clear how we can best translate our familiar physical-world-based moral concepts into a virtual realm. Do virtual entities and events have the same moral status or significance as their real-world counterparts? Do virtual achievements count for anything? Even if they count for something, do they count as much as real ones? Is virtual adultery a real betrayal? Is virtual theft a crime? And so on.

In our affluent world, where participation in semi-virtual realities is a voluntary, optional leisure activity, the 'ethical dilemmas' of a virtual world can seem comparatively trivial. So long as the terms and conditions are clear and there is no false advertising, why not just let people choose whatever solipsist or interpersonal experience machines they want? (Utilitarians might embrace this freedom of choice for familiar Millian liberal reasons.) The ethical stakes are much higher if the external world is broken. If everyone *must* inhabit *some* experience machine, and especially if (for technical or social reasons) we must all inhabit *the same interpersonal experience machine*, then future ethics must adapt to a world where human control over our shared environment extends much further than ever before.

As we will now see, other technological futures introduce new complications.

3.5 Well-Being and Digital Futures

Recall our *digital future* where flesh-and-blood humans have been replaced by digital beings – intelligent machines and/or digital copies of human brains.

Digital futures are credible. No one can reasonably be confident that this won't happen. We should be wary of breathless predictions of the imminent rise of super-intelligent machines (see, e.g., the critique presented in Floridi, 2014). But confident pronouncements that artificial intelligence and digital uploading will forever remain engineering impossibilities are equally suspect. Computers continually confound their critics by performing tasks long deemed 'impossible'. ('No computer will ever play checkers or chess or Go, drive a car, recognise a face', etc.)

Digital futures could be especially appealing to people whose 'real-world' alternative is already broken or virtual. A future generation already inhabiting a virtual environment might opt to 'upload' to a fully digital virtual world. Or future people might face an earlier choice between broken and digital futures. (Perhaps only digital beings can survive some catastrophe that will destroy both real-world creatures and non-uploaded virtual life. Or perhaps we have sufficient resources to upload, store, and 'run' a billion minds but not to preserve a comparable number of brains-in-vats.) Future people must also choose between many *different* digital futures. (Should they opt for destructive uploading or digital copying or the development of non-human-based artificial digital intelligences? And which *form* of uploading or copying or AI is best?)

The digital future presents itself as a utopian post-scarcity alternative to the broken future. Digital futures could be wonderful. Digital beings might all enjoy spectacularly rich lives. But digital futures could also be empty, broken, or otherwise very negative. Although it seems to be a trans-humanist paradise, every digital future has the potential to very rapidly descend into a particularly unpleasant broken future where resources are insufficient to support all existing digital beings and the price of labour falls far below the cost of keeping any flesh-and-blood human worker alive. This is due to the threat of a digital population explosion. Unlike human beings, whose reproduction is limited by biology, natural resources, and inclination, digital beings can reproduce at will. And they may have strong incentives to do so. For instance, Robin Hanson speculates that, in a competitive market, 'emulations' based on a few thousand 'exceptional' humans could both dominate the digital economy and effortlessly outcompete human labour – perhaps by selling short-lived copies that do a full day's work and then expire without enjoying any leisure time (Hanson, 2016). Flesh-and-blood humans could be overwhelmed by a population explosion that, from their (comparatively slow) human perspective, would seem more or less instantaneous (Bostrom, 2014, pp. 22–51).

Like ordinary humans, *digital* beings could be psychopathic or otherwise morally unreliable. Indeed, this is quite likely, for several reasons: it may be much easier to engineer artificial agents who don't respond to moral reasons than ones who do (Bostrom, 2014, pp. 105–14), psychopathic or morally unreliable humans may be more likely to have both the resources and the inclination to upload and multiply themselves, and the uploading process itself might undermine a person's concern for their fellow humans (along with their sanity). The twin threats of digital population explosion and morally unreliable digital beings exacerbate one another. If digital reproduction is constrained only by internalised moral norms, then a single morally unreliable digital being could very quickly dominate a law-abiding population!

Another worrying possibility is a mixed digital future where digital beings co-exist with ordinary non-digital humans. How will flesh-and-blood humans interact with digital beings? In particular, can human beings compete with much faster and smarter digital beings? Or will unenhanced humans be entirely at the mercy of superior digital beings? This scenario might be very good for humans *if* digital beings are well-disposed to us and understand our needs. But what if they are hostile, indifferent, or simply mistaken about what is good for us?

A final threat is that a digital future might be empty rather than broken. One especially disturbing prospect is an *unconscious* digital future, where both intelligent machines and digital humans lack any phenomenological experience, inner life, or 'qualia'. Perhaps, in J. J. Valberg's apt phrase, unlike each of us, no digital being finds itself at the centre of an 'arena of presence' (Valberg, 2007). This future is also credible. Consciousness could turn out to be simply a matter of patterns of information processing – something machines could easily share. But it might instead be an emergent feature specific to our biology. Experts – whether scientific, religious, or philosophical – disagree (contrast, e.g., Hofstadter, 2007 and Searle, 1997). The question of machine consciousness is a site of reasonable philosophical disagreement. Perhaps consciousness and intelligence do always go together. (They may even turn out to be the same thing.) But, for all anyone knows, they may sometimes come apart. It is therefore worth asking what would follow if they did. Conscious digital entities are a stock device in science fiction, as is the specific trope of copying a person into a computer. A presumption of digital consciousness dominates popular culture. My unconscious digital future is counter-intuitive. But that is a reason to explore it, not a reason to ignore it.

If digital beings lack whatever makes human lives matter, then the digital future is empty. The empty digital future most clearly arises if both (1) the digital future is unconscious and (2) consciousness is a necessary condition for possessing a life that matters. Most obviously, if hedonism is correct, then entities who cannot experience pleasure and pain cannot possibly have lives worth living. Other accounts of well-being could also yield an empty digital future. For instance, if our animal nature is somehow essential to the value of

our lives, then digital beings (and especially uploaded copies of human origi-
nals) would lack value even if they were conscious.

Digital futures raise many different questions for utilitarian future ethics. Is
the unconscious digital future desirable? If it is bad, how bad is it? Would an
unconscious digital future be a catastrophe on a par with human extinction, or
can any lost value be replaced? For instance, suppose digital beings differ from
humans in two ways: they lack any capacity for physical embodiment or
enjoyment, but they possess a much greater capacity for intellectual achievement. Could the former deficiency be outweighed by the latter advantage? If we
are risk-averse, is the unconscious digital future the worst possibility – something to be avoided at all costs? Or are there other digital futures that would be
worse? (Imagine a future where billions of digital simulations are tortured for
the pleasure or profit of a tiny minority of fabulously wealthy digital
oligarchs . . .)

The controversy here is both metaphysical and normative. Suppose we are
contemplating the transition to a digital future and we ask whether that transition is likely to *succeed*. Obviously, a successful digital transition requires
technological sophistication. But what *counts* as a *successful* digital transition
also depends on what is most *important* about flesh-and-blood human life. And
that is a normative question. We saw earlier that objectivists complain that
hedonists cannot see what is missing in virtual futures. In digital futures, the risk
is reversed. If objectivism is true, then unconscious intelligent machines might
have access to (some) genuine objective values despite lacking any phenomenological experience. But if hedonism is true, then *any* unconscious future is
necessarily a valueless void. If we presuppose either the wrong metaphysics or
the wrong story about value, we risk the annihilation of value itself.

The contrast between hedonism and objective list theory may not be as stark
as this. Many objectivists will agree with the hedonist claim that the unconscious digital future is a valueless void. For instance, if other list items (such as
achievement, knowledge, friendship, or preference satisfaction) can only possibly add value to a person's life if they *experience* them, there can be no
valuable lives in a world without experiences. However, other objectivists will
find some value in the unconscious digital future – because *some* items on their
lists are *not* subject to any experience requirement. (Perhaps some achievements
matter even if one is not consciously aware of them.) In this hybrid view,
unconscious digital futures could outweigh worlds with flesh-and-blood
humans by accumulating a sufficient quantity of valuable achievements to
compensate for their inhabitants' lack of awareness. Given the potentially
enormous scope for digital explosion and achievement, this is not out of the
question.

The unconscious digital future is thus a good test case for experience requirements within objective list theory. If we are confident that any unconscious digital future *must* be a valueless void, then we conclude that *all* list items are subject to an experience requirement. On the other hand, if we are more confident that some list items are *not* subject to any experience requirement, then we will bite the bullet and insist that the deficiencies of an unconscious digital future could in principle be outweighed.

The prospect of a digital future also raises worries about the moral status of animals. Will animals be uploaded or replicated digitally? If so, will those digital animals be conscious? Or will digital beings simply fail to recognise or understand the value of non-rational sentient lives? (Just as they might fail to see the point of biological humans!) This parallels a debate we saw earlier in relation to virtual futures. While all contemporary utilitarians recognise the significance of non-human animal well-being, many technological futures threaten to eliminate non-human animals altogether. In a virtual, digital, or extraterrestrial future, there is no *human* need (and probably no space) for non-human animals. Is the absence of non-human animal well-being a negative feature of these possible futures? If so, how should we weigh it against their positive aspects?

The digital future also introduces a new ethical dilemma regarding the *scope* of well-being. Should utilitarians recognise digital beings as moral agents, persons, or potential sites of value? (Mulgan, 2014a.) One popular *moral* reading of science fiction identifies moral progress with a broadening of ethical concern to embrace people of all religions, races, and genders, and even other sentient terrestrial animals – and then invites us to further expand our ethical circle to include aliens and digital beings.

We could interpret this presumption of digital significance as a *moral* imperative rather than a metaphysical hypothesis: 'Always treat intelligent machines as conscious and morally significant beings, because otherwise you risk treating conscious digital *people* as if they were merely unconscious *things*!' There is no comparable risk on the other side. It doesn't really matter if you mistakenly treat a toaster as if it were a person. (Unless this mistake leads you to sacrifice important human interests to protect the imaginary 'interests' of toasters.) This suggests that even if conscious and unconscious digital futures are both credible, we should always assume the former.

The presumption of digital significance mirrors familiar utilitarian arguments about animals. Suppose someone tells you that boiling animal X alive before you eat it would provide you with a unique and pleasurable sensation. If you are not sure whether or not animal X can feel pain while it is being boiled alive, then you should err on the side of caution. It is better to avoid torturing a sentient being than to forego a possibly innocent pleasure.

The presumption of moral significance makes sense for animals that already exist. Similarly, it would be the right approach if we encountered *already existing* digital beings on some distant planet. But once we ask whether to *create* digital beings, and especially whether humans should *transform themselves* into digital beings, then things are much less obvious. There are now very significant risks *on both sides*. If we falsely assume that our digital descendants are *un*conscious, then we risk losing vast improvements in human well-being or mistreating real moral persons. But if we falsely assume that digital beings *are* conscious when they are not, we risk the total annihilation of human value. (After all, unconscious intelligent machines will probably regard consciousness – 'whatever that is!' – as unimportant. If they take over, they may remove consciousness without thinking twice.) This is a new ethical predicament, because no credible future raises analogous doubts about other expansions of ethical concern. We don't have similar worries that animals will turn out not to be sentient.

Like the virtual future, the digital future thus puts pressure on utilitarian assumptions about the content and scope of well-being.

The different ways that debates about well-being might be transformed in various broken, virtual, and digital futures highlights the extent of our uncertainty about the future – along both empirical and normative dimensions. (We don't know what will happen in the distant future, but we also don't know whether or not some particular possible future would be desirable.) Section 4.5 asks whether this uncertainty renders utilitarians clueless in future ethics. Sections 4.1 to 4.4 first ask whether the resources developed in earlier sections enable utilitarians to shed new light on some perennial puzzles in contemporary future ethics.

4 Some Puzzles in Contemporary Future Ethics

Contemporary future ethics focuses on a series of puzzles introduced by Parfit's *Reasons and Persons*. In this section, we ask how collective utilitarians might re-think those puzzles.

4.1 Totalism and Its Rivals

Suppose you could create any possible world with any possible population. As a utilitarian, which world should you choose? Because they base morality on the pursuit of the best possible consequences, utilitarians must answer this question. Utilitarians need a theory of aggregation – taking us from the values of individual lives to the values of possible populations.

Contemporary discussion begins with two distinctions from Parfit. The first is between *Same People Choices* (where our choice affects people who will exist whatever we do) and *Different People Choices* (where our choice determines which future people there will be). Parfit argues that Different People Choices are more common than we normally think and that this gives utilitarianism a prima facie advantage over its rivals. Parfit then divides Different People Choices into *Same Number Choices* (where our choice affects who exists but not how many people exist) and *Different Number Choices* (where our choice affects how many people exist) (Parfit, 1984, p. 356). As we'll see in section 4.2, Different *People* Choices are problematic for non-utilitarians. Unfortunately, Different *Number* Choices raise many new difficulties for utilitarianism.

Historically, the utilitarian tradition offers two main accounts of aggregation. Under totalism, the best outcome is the one that contains the greatest *total* happiness. Under averagism, the best outcome contains the highest *average* level of happiness. The classical utilitarians did not always clearly distinguish these views. This is understandable, as the two views must coincide in Same Number Choices. (For any two populations of the same size, the one with higher total well-being also has the higher average.) But the two views often come apart in Different Number Choices. Consider a choice between one possible future where a large population enjoys moderate happiness and another where fewer people are very much happier. Suppose the first future has greater total happiness while the second has higher average happiness. Which future is better *in terms of human happiness*?

A central issue for totalism is the location of the *zero level*. Most utilitarians agree that some possible human lives are *worth living* and others are *not worth living*. They also agree that many past and present *actual* human lives fall into each category. If we imagine arranging possible human lives on a scale of goodness, the zero level is the point where lives go from positive (worth living) to negative (not worth living). A healthy affluent life lasting a hundred years, filled with many achievements, friendships, and pleasures seems clearly worth living. And a life containing *nothing* but agony would be not worth living. The idea of a zero level is crucial to totalism because each new life adds value if and only if it is above zero. As we shall see in section 4.2, the distinction between lives that are worth living and those that are not worth living is also central to procreative ethics.

4.1.1 Parfit's Repugnant Conclusion

Totalism is the simplest theory of aggregation, and it has been the most popular view among philosophers. (Economists, by contrast, have often favoured averagism.) The basic argument for totalism is simple. If we value happiness, then presumably we should aim to produce as much happiness as possible. However, totalism has some very unappealing implications. The most famous objection to totalism dates back to Henry Sidgwick, and it takes its modern name from Parfit (Sidgwick, 1907, pp. 415–16; Parfit, 1984, p. 388).

The Repugnant Conclusion. For any possible population of at least ten billion people, all with a very high quality of life, there must be some much larger imaginable population whose existence, if other things are equal, would be better, even though its members have lives that are barely worth living.

To see why totalism implies the Repugnant Conclusion, begin with a world (A) where ten billion people all have extremely good lives. Imagine a second world (B), with more than twice as many people, each of whom is only half as happy as the people in A. Total happiness in B exceeds that in A. Now repeat this process until we reach a world (Z) where a vast population have lives barely worth living. As each step increases total happiness, Z must be better than A.

Parfit finds this result 'intrinsically repugnant' (Parfit, 1984, p. 390). If totalism yields this conclusion, then it is unacceptable. The Repugnant Conclusion is a classic example of a thought experiment that allegedly constitutes a decisive counter-example to a philosophical view. It is one of the organising problems of contemporary utilitarian future ethics (see, e.g., Ryberg and Tannsjo, 2004). This is partly because, for many utilitarians, future ethics is just the search for Parfit's elusive 'Theory X' (the correct account of aggregation)! Many utilitarians begin their discussion of future ethics by saying how they will deal with the Repugnant Conclusion – rejecting either totalism itself or Parfit's intuition that A is better than Z.

It is tempting to reject intuitions altogether. As philosophers, we should ask whether a conclusion follows from well-established premises, not whether it 'appears' repugnant. But can we really dispense with intuitions entirely? What *else* could ground our *normative* premises? When philosophers say that they reject intuitions, this usually means that they reject some intuitions in favour of others. Some *non*-utilitarians will claim that they can dispense with intuitions about the comparative values of possible futures altogether and simply refuse to say whether A is better or worse than Z. It is doubtful whether even the most anti-utilitarian philosopher could do without *any* intuitions of comparative value. (How else will they decide which possible future to aim at?) However, what is not in doubt is that *utilitarians* clearly cannot take this route. They must offer *some* theory of aggregation.

A second obvious alternative is to replace totalism. Unfortunately, most alternatives to totalism face other, equally daunting, objections. Consider averagism. This view easily avoids the Repugnant Conclusion. World A contains much higher average happiness than Z. But averagism faces its own objections. Many are variations of the *hermit problem*. Suppose everyone in the cosmos is extremely happy. We create a new person on a distant uninhabited planet. (Let's call that person 'Hermit'.) Hermit's life, while very good, is slightly below the cosmic average. Averagism insists that our creation of Hermit makes things worse. Even more problematically, averagism implies that whether or not we ought to create Hermit depends on the happiness of people in distant corners of the cosmos with whom Hermit will never interact. (If everyone else had been less happy, then our creation of Hermit – exactly as they are – would have improved things.) Both claims seem implausible. As Parfit puts it, the 'mere addition' of lives worth living cannot make things worse, and our moral decisions should not depend on how happy the ancient Egyptians were (Parfit, 1984, p. 420).

The hermit problem plays a similar dialectical role to the Repugnant Conclusion. Defenders of averagism must either defend these odd implications or deny that their theory implies them. One popular response is to limit our calculation of average happiness to those affected by our actions – thus removing the need to consider the welfare of very distant people. But this still leaves Parfit's *mere addition objection*. Any proponent of averagism must bite the bullet and agree that the addition of any person with below-average happiness does make things *worse* – even if their life is very worthwhile. Most utilitarians find this even harder to accept than the Repugnant Conclusion.[14]

Another popular account of aggregation is the lexical view (Parfit, 1986; Mulgan, 2006, chapter 3). Suppose you enjoy both Mozart and Muzak. Someone offers you a choice between one day of Mozart and as much Muzak as you like. If you opt for the former – perhaps because *no amount* of Muzak could match the smallest amount of Mozart – then you believe that Mozart is *lexically superior* to Muzak. Similarly, the lexical view holds that some possible human lives are lexically superior to others.

The lexical view can avoid the Repugnant Conclusion. Suppose the creatures in A and Z belong to different species. Perhaps A contains flourishing human beings while Z is full of slugs. If we place the lexical level between flourishing human lives and ordinary slug lives, then A is better than Z, because ten billion human lives are more valuable than any number of slug lives. More

---

[14] The literature contains many other theories of aggregation designed to fill the space between totalism and averagism (Parfit, 1984, chapters 19 and 20; Greaves, 2017). However, I argue elsewhere that these all either share the fate of averagism (Mulgan, 2001a) or fall foul of a *Reverse Repugnant Conclusion*, where a world (call it A-minus) where ten billion people live long lives of unalloyed excruciating agony is better than another world (Z-minus) where a vast number of people have lives which are almost but not quite worth living (Mulgan, 2002). Any attempt to render the Repugnant Conclusion more palatable by raising the zero level – and thereby improving the quality of life in Parfit's original Z world – makes the *Reverse* Repugnant Conclusion even less palatable.

controversially, a lexical view could also hold that ten billion flourishing human lives trump *any* number of human lives that are barely worth living. A could thus be better than Z even if both contain only human beings.

One pressing problem for any lexical view is Parfit's *continuum objection*.

> Mozart and Muzak ... seem to be in quite different categories. But there is a fairly smooth continuum between these two. Though Haydn is not as good as Mozart, he is very good. And there is other music which is not far below Haydn's, other music not far below this, and so on. Similar claims apply to the ... other things which give most to the value of life. ... Since this is so, it may be hard to defend the view that what is best has more value than any amount of what is nearly as good. (Parfit, 1986, p. 164.)

The lexical view must tell us where to draw the line – and why. How do we decide which possible *human* lives are above the lexical threshold and which are below? Because the practical implications of the lexical view depend very largely on where we set the threshold, these are very significant decisions.

Totalism, averagism, and the lexical view all completely ignore the *distribution* of well-being. *Egalitarians* object that two outcomes with identical total and average well-being might differ in value because one has a more equal distribution. Egalitarianism notoriously faces *levelling-down objections*. It seems perverse to increase equality in ways that benefit no one, such as deliberately reducing the well-being of the better-off. (Consider a striking example. Some people are blind. If we blind all the sighted people, then we have made things 'equal regarding sightedness'. But is this any kind of improvement?) *Prioritarians* seek to preserve the insights of egalitarianism while avoiding levelling-down problems. They argue that adding worthwhile lives always makes things better, but we should give priority to improving the well-being of those who are worst off (Parfit, 1991; Holtug, 2010).

Totalists agree that equality often has *instrumental value*. The most equal distribution of *resources* might maximise *welfare* due to diminishing marginal utility, while an unequal distribution of any good might yield less total welfare due to the negative impact of envy or resentment. However, totalists insist that equality has no *independent value*. Here we seem to reach another intuitive bedrock.

These debates are ongoing. This is partly because no theory avoids counter-intuitive results. Indeed, a number of philosophers have defended 'impossibility theorems', which demonstrate that no *possible* theory of aggregation can meet all of a small set of intuitively compelling axioms (e.g., Arrhenius, forthcoming). One response to these impossibility results is to retain totalism on the basis of its theoretical simplicity and then downplay its counter-intuitive results by noting that our moral intuitions are ill-suited to deal with imaginary cases involving very large numbers. But it is fair to say that, thirty years after Parfit issued his challenge to find Theory X, every theory of aggregation has more opponents than supporters.

The debate about aggregation typically contrasts different populations of *non-enhanced biological humans*. As we saw earlier, utilitarian future ethics must also consider the well-being of non-human terrestrial animals, digital beings, and extraterrestrials. Introducing non-human welfare has several impacts on debates about aggregation. For instance, Parfit's Repugnant Conclusion intuition is perhaps most compelling when the populations in A and Z belong to very different species, as in my earlier example contrasting slugs and humans; and digital beings – whose intellectual sophistication might literally come in degrees – may eventually provide a real-life example of Parfit's continuum argument against the lexical view.

Non-human beings also raise interesting issues concerning mere addition. If we assume totalism, then the future is better if it contains (happy) non-human animals and digital beings *as well as happy humans* – even if the happiness of each individual animal or digital being is minimal. How do we factor in all the value that might be contained in the lives of non-human individuals? (Does the expected future value of microbial life or very minimal digital existence exceed the expected future value of human life? This raises the spectre of a new Repugnant Conclusion. Such beings *might* each contain *some* positive value, and there are enormous numbers of them, therefore . . .) By contrast, averagists might prefer a future without *any* animals or low-level digital beings, because they would reduce average well-being. On the other hand, if digital beings are *superior* to humans, then *we* will be the ones dragging down the cosmic average!

Non-human well-being also delivers another blow against egalitarianism and prioritarianism. It is very hard to retain a commitment to the independent value of equality (or even priority) when we factor in animals or digital beings. Is there *any* reason to give priority to raising the well-being of minimally happy slugs or barely conscious computer programmes rather than incomparably happier humans? This suggests that equality is something that applies, if at all, only between members of the same species or community. But totalists will argue that this unnecessarily complicates our utilitarian theory, and it is better to regard equality as merely instrumentally valuable.

It is easy to dismiss these puzzles of aggregation as theoretical curiosities. But they could have real-world implications. Virtual, digital, and extraterrestrial futures, in particular, all look very different to the totalist than to the averagist.

4.1.2 Aggregation for Collective Utilitarians

I will argue that collective utilitarian theories such as rule or ideal outlook utilitarianism offer a possible solution to these impasses. These theories distinguish between the *foundational values* used to select our ideal code of rules or moral outlook and *evaluations within* that code or outlook itself. When we ask what someone who had internalised the ideal moral outlook would feel free to do, we are inevitably also asking what they *value*. In principle, a theory's *internalised* values and *foundational* values might diverge. Indeed, we should expect this. If our ideal code or outlook does not collapse into a single act consequentialist rule ('Always do the act with the best consequences.'), then it must include some non-consequentialist rules, distinctions, and priorities. It would be surprising if it didn't also include some non-foundational *values*. Perhaps our foundational values are totalist, but the outlook that maximises total value incorporates either a concern for average welfare, a lexical level, or a commitment to prioritising the well-being of the worst-off.

The flexibility of collective utilitarianism allows us to re-examine our intuitive reactions to Parfit's thought experiments. Many people have stronger intuitions regarding our *obligations* to future people than they do about the *comparative values* of possible futures. For instance, rejection of the Repugnant Conclusion might be motivated not by the abstract claim that Z is worse than A but by the thought that the inhabitants of A are not obliged to transform their world into Z. Suppose we are living in Parfit's A. You tell me that, after examining the esoteric philosophical literature on population ethics, aggregation, and axiology, you are convinced that Z is impersonally better than A. I find this counter-intuitive. However, I realise that intuitions about large numbers are unreliable and that every axiology is intuitively problematic. I might disagree, but I don't think your view is ridiculous. You then say that, because Z is better than A, we *are morally obliged to transform our flourishing A world* into a miserable version of Parfit's Z world. I might well regard this as a step too far!

Act utilitarians cannot separate these two thoughts. Anyone who has a choice between two possible futures *must* opt for the better one. But because it severs the tight connection between value and right action, collective utilitarianism can agree that no one is obliged to *choose* Z over A – without thereby automatically concluding that Z is not better than A.

The distinction between foundational values and internalised values allows collective utilitarians to make two different dialectical moves. First, different foundational values may converge on the same ideal outlook or code. Despite their theoretical differences, totalists might agree with averagists, or hedonists with objectivists. Collective utilitarians could then remain completely agnostic regarding the foundational question. Second, even when different foundational values yield different ideal outlooks or codes, collective utilitarians can recognise the intuitive appeal of competing accounts of value by combining (say) a totalist account of foundational values with a more diverse set of internal values. Collective utilitarians who take this second route must still select one (controversial) account of foundational values, but they do avoid many of its counter-intuitive consequences, as we have just seen in relation to the Repugnant Conclusion.

In the rest of this section, I argue that, by borrowing familiar non-utilitarian moral distinctions, collective utilitarians can accommodate many other features of common sense future ethics such as procreative freedom and the procreative asymmetry. Collective utilitarians can also incorporate into their theory of right action elements borrowed from *competing theories of aggregation* – such as lexical thresholds or a focus on average well-being – even if their foundational values remain totalist.

The moral code or outlook that best promotes total happiness may encourage individual agents to depart from totalism in their moral deliberations – just as it encourages them to depart from act consequentialism. For instance, a society might set itself the policy goal of maximising the *average* quality of life of its grandchildren. Alternatively, borrowing from egalitarianism or prioritarianism, collective total utilitarians might argue that, while an equal distribution of well-being has no greater value than an unequal one *at the level of foundational value*, our ideal moral outlook will include a moral disposition to seek an equal distribution of well-being. For a variety of reasons, things go better overall (even by totalist lights) if we all strive for equality and fairness.

Another example, which I explore elsewhere at length, is that a lexical view might be a useful way to interpret a *practical obligation* to raise everyone in a given society above a certain threshold (Mulgan, 2004, 2006, p. 174). This new *internal* lexical threshold would be *context-dependent*. Its precise location will differ from one deliberative context to another. Placing our lexical level *within* the ideal moral outlook also allows us to sidestep Parfit's seemingly devastating continuum objection. If we treat the lexical threshold as a stance to be adopted in particular deliberative contexts, rather than an objective feature of our foundational theory of comparative value, then it is easier to vary it.

The shift to a context-dependent lexical level is especially helpful in the transition to a *broken future*. Within the ideal moral outlook, the lexical threshold represents a worthwhile life that is *guaranteed* to everyone – a protected moral sphere where each individual is both morally and practically free to concentrate on their own projects, goals, and relationships even at the expense of aggregate well-being. However, in a broken world, where favourable conditions have been lost, no one can reasonably insist on the broad range of resource-intensive goals which, over the past few centuries, we have built into our *affluent interpretation* of the lexical threshold. More drastically, if it is not possible for everyone to survive, then there is *nothing* that can meaningfully be guaranteed to everyone.

Rather than abandoning the lexical threshold, however, future collective utilitarians will instead *re-imagine* it. They might begin with the notion of a fair and equal *chance* of surviving (or living a worthwhile life) and then insist that this *fair chance* is what must be guaranteed to all. Consider one simple case. If an equal share of water is insufficient for survival, it makes no sense to give everyone an equal inadequate share rather than an equal *chance* of an adequate share.

Once again, we see that utilitarianism has a flexibility that non-utilitarian accounts of rights lack. Today, perhaps with good utilitarian reasons, we regard the violation of basic human rights as unthinkable. In my terminology: we build inviolable rights into our lexical threshold. But this unbending notion of rights breaks apart in a truly broken world. Inflexible non-utilitarian rights will simply be abandoned. By contrast, a *utilitarian* account of rights bends to fit this new (unfortunate) context. A broken world alters both the content and the strength of rights. The best utilitarian political institutions may reluctantly have to shift from securing everyone's survival to managing a fair distribution of chances to survive.

This completes our brief discussion of utilitarian aggregation. We now turn to other puzzles in contemporary future ethics.

4.2 Parfit's Non-identity Problem and Procreative Asymmetries

Parfit's central challenge for non-utilitarians is the *Non-identity Problem*. Parfit argues that, because they are designed for Same People Choices, many non-utilitarian theories cope poorly with Different People Choices (Parfit, 1984, p. 356). This matters because Different People Choices are more frequent than we realise. In Parfit's own Risky Policy example, we bury nuclear waste where there is a significant earthquake risk in the distant future (Parfit, 1984, p. 371). Many centuries later, an earthquake releases radiation, killing thousands of people. Intuitively, our choice is wrong because we harm those who die. But if our initial choice influences patterns of migration and social interaction over several generations, then any particular individual who is killed by the future catastrophe would never have existed at all if we had chosen differently. Their parents would never have met – indeed, their parents might never have existed themselves. Our choice thus harms no one. You cannot harm someone if they would otherwise never exist, and it would be bizarre to say that we harm the non-existent possible people who would have enjoyed better lives if we had chosen the safe policy. How can you harm someone who *never* exists?

Parfit's non-identity problem targets *person-affecting theories*, which insist that actions are only wrong if some particular person is worse off than they would otherwise have been. Many non-utilitarian theories are person-affecting. Consider the social contract tradition, where justice is modelled as a bargain or agreement among rational individuals. How can we begin to imagine contracts, bargains, or co-operative schemes involving future people whose existence and identity depend upon what we decide? Contractualists as diverse as Immanuel Kant, John Rawls, David Gauthier, and T. M. Scanlon all face serious difficulties here (see, e.g., Gosseries and Meyer, 2009).

By contrast, utilitarians can sidestep non-identity, endorse Parfit's *No Difference View*, and treat Same and Different People Choices identically (Parfit, 1984, p. 367). What matters is how happy future people will be, not who they are. It is wrong to choose Parfit's Risky Policy because this produces a less happy future. Discovering that we face a Different People Choice makes no moral difference.

The non-identity problem is a central puzzle in the emerging philosophical literature on procreative ethics. Procreative ethics is a difficult topic for both utilitarians and non-utilitarians. In a liberal society, we naturally regard individual procreative decisions as private and beyond the reach of ethics. However, bringing a person into existence obviously has a huge impact on their well-being. Utilitarians therefore cannot avoid subjecting such decisions to ethical scrutiny.

Contemporary philosophical procreative ethics can be organised around puzzles generated by three intuitively appealing but conflicting claims (e.g., McMahan, 2013; Roberts, 2011):

- **Negative Obligation:** It is always (very) wrong to knowingly create a person whose life will be worth not living (i.e., below the zero level).
- **No Positive Obligation:** There is no obligation to create a person whose life would be well worth living.
- **General Permission:** Conventional human procreation is (at least) morally permissible in ordinary circumstances.

The first two claims constitute the *procreative asymmetry*. The first challenge for any procreative ethic is to either accept (and explain) this apparent asymmetry or explain it away. Those who accept the asymmetry face a second challenge, as our first two claims are in tension with the third. If deliberately creating an unhappy person is always very wrong, and if no one is obliged to have children even if they are very confident that the person they would create would be very happy, then surely human procreation is always at least morally problematic. How can we justify an activity that risks something bad and promises something neutral? Yet most people are *very* confident that our current standard practice of creating new persons is morally unproblematic.

Utilitarians have a simple solution. They can accept the negative obligation and general permission claims and reject the no positive obligation claim. Other things being equal, adding a life not worth living makes things worse overall. This provides a compelling utilitarian reason against adding such lives. Other things being equal, failing to add a good life has the same overall impact as adding an equivalently bad life below zero. Both actions are *equally wrong*. Although there may be asymmetries in practice if other things are not equal, there is no *intrinsic* asymmetry. This is a striking illustration of utilitarianism's general rejection of familiar common sense asymmetries and distinctions. For the utilitarian, human procreation is permissible if and only if it promotes happiness overall. Whether this corresponds to the procreative permissions of common sense morality is another matter.

While many utilitarians do favour both Parfit's No Difference View and the standard utilitarian response to procreative asymmetry, *collective* utilitarians can be more flexible. They can reject Parfit's Risky Policy but still recognise some moral difference between Same and Different People Choices. If the moral outlook that best promotes future well-being recognises *both* a general reason to promote the good *and* obligations to specific individuals, then someone who has internalised that outlook may feel stronger obligations to raise the well-being of people who already exist (or future people who will exist whatever the agent now does) than to create equally happy *extra* people. This flexibility brings collective utilitarianism closer to common sense morality. It is especially useful in constructing a utilitarian procreative ethic.

Before we explore the resources of collective utilitarianism, however, we first explore a more radical utilitarian alternative.

4.3 Person-Affecting Utilitarianism

Modern utilitarianism is explicitly both impersonal and consequentialist. Moral evaluation is based on promoting the impersonal value of outcomes. However, it is not clear that the classical founders of utilitarianism shared these modern commitments. Nor is it obvious that impersonalism and consequentialism are essential components of utilitarianism. Suppose we agree that the *defining* commitment of utilitarianism is that morality is about promoting human happiness. As Jan Narveson observed, there are two ways to do this: by making happy people or by making people happy (Narveson, 1967). More recently, Melinda Roberts has defended a *person-affecting consequentialism* where, instead of maximising total happiness, we aim to maximise the happiness of each individual (Roberts, 2002, 2007, 2011).

Roberts posits the following *necessary* condition for wrongness: an action is wrong only if it harms someone, where a person is harmed if and only if they are worse off than they could otherwise have been. Roberts's notion of harm is very inclusive. I harm someone whenever I fail to maximise their lifetime well-being – whenever some other act of mine would have given them a better life. If I don't give all my money to some billionaire, I harm them! In Same People Choices, we cannot avoid harming at least one person. Therefore, other conditions must come to the fore. Harm cannot be sufficient for wrongness. However, Roberts's necessary condition is significant for procreative ethics. If I create someone and I *could not* have given them a better life, then I do *not* harm them. In this case, according to Roberts, my action cannot be wrong.

Roberts's view may seem very implausible. Consider a striking example from Gregory Kavka (Kavka, 1982). A heterosexual couple decide to have a child so that they can sell them into slavery in order to raise money to buy a luxury yacht. Suppose (rather implausibly) the couple are sure that, despite being a slave, their child's life will be worth living overall. As they would not otherwise have existed at all, this child is not *worse-off than they would otherwise have been*. Therefore, according to Roberts, the parents do nothing wrong!

Roberts replies that Kavka's slave parents *do* act wrongly because they could have given their child a much better life. They didn't have to sell the child into slavery! The relevant question is whether they *could* have given the child a better life, not what they *would* have done. Roberts offers the following analogy. Suppose I shoot you in the leg. You complain that I have harmed you. I reply that I was so angry – and I am so incapable of controlling myself – that if I hadn't shot you in the leg, I would have shot you in the head. If I hadn't shot you in the leg, you would have been *worse off* than you are now. Therefore, I have not harmed you. You would find this excuse very unconvincing. Surely I *could* – and should – have refrained from shooting you at all.

More generally, Roberts distinguishes three types of non-identity problem.

1 **Won't Do Better:** The extra person has a sub-optimal life because the agent is *unwilling* to give them a better life. The classic example is Kavka's slave child case. Kavka's parents harm their child because they fail to give them the best life they could.

2 **Can't Expect Better:** The extra person has a good life and their existence was highly contingent. The agent argues that if they had done something else, this person would almost certainly not have existed. As the person's life is worth living, they cannot claim to have been harmed. A classic example is Parfit's Risky Policy. Roberts argues that the agent's defence in these cases trades on an ambiguity between ex ante and ex post evaluation. We can separate the features of the present action that give the extra person a sub-optimal life from the features that are directly identity-determining for them. Therefore, there must be some alternative action available to the agent which both (a) offered the same ex ante probability that *this particular extra person* would come into existence and also (b) would have given that person a better life if they did exist. This alternative action thus offers *this particular extra person* greater ex ante *expected* well-being, and therefore the agent has harmed them. For instance, if we implement Parfit's Risky Policy, there is *some* safe alternative that would have the same identity-determining impacts without the accompanying risk of future catastrophe.

3 **Can't Do Better:** The agent has no possible alternative action that could have given the extra person a better life. The classic example is cases involving disabilities that are essentially linked to a person's genetic identity. Roberts argues that these are the *real* non-identity cases. It is only in these cases that the extra person is not harmed.

In Won't Do Better and Can't Expect Better cases, Roberts argues that harm does occur, and therefore our actions can be wrong. In Can't Do Better cases, she bites the bullet and denies both that the future person has been wronged and that there are any other grounds for concluding that the agent's action is wrong. So long as we ensure that every future person has the best possible life they could have enjoyed, our actions are not morally criticisable.

Roberts's view is controversial. Suppose you have a choice between creating a healthy child and a disabled child, where the latter's disability is identity-determining for them. (In other words, that particular child *could not possibly* exist without suffering that disability.) According to Roberts, if you take the second option, then you do not harm your child, and therefore your action cannot be wrong (unless it happens to harm someone else).

In section 4.4, I argue that collective utilitarians can steer a middle path between act utilitarianism and person-affecting consequentialism.

4.4 A Collective Utilitarian Procreative Ethic

As with Parfit's No Difference View, many people find the act utilitarian response to procreative asymmetry too extreme. But few people would go to the other extreme and agree that it is always wrong to have children. Fortunately, collective utilitarianism offers a moderate alternative. On the one hand, any utilitarian procreative ethic will include a strong reason to promote the good, thus generating *some* prima facie reason to have a happy child (cf. Chappell, 2017). On the other hand, there are limits to the demands of any collective utilitarianism. Moral outlooks that are *too* demanding, impersonal, or alien could not be effectively internalised by human beings or handed down the generations. Both rule and ideal outlook utilitarianism recognise a broad sphere of personal moral freedom (including procreative freedom) where agents are free to *not* maximally promote the good. Also, notwithstanding our foundational commitment to impersonal value, the ideal code or outlook may also include person-affecting principles, non-consequentialist distinctions like doing and allowing, priority of actual people over future people, and a rejection of procreative coercion. Someone who had internalised that ideal outlook would not feel obliged to create the happiest children they possibly could – let alone the possible children whose existence would maximise *other people's happiness* (Mulgan, 2006, pp. 172–3).

In my 2006 book *Future People*, I argued that collective utilitarianism can accommodate intuitively plausible principles such as the following:

1 **Wrongness:** It is wrong to gratuitously create a child whose life contains nothing but suffering or a child whose life is much worse than it could have been (e.g., by deliberately giving one's child a disability) (Mulgan, 2006, p. 5).
2 **Liberty:** People should enjoy broad moral, practical, political, social, and legal freedom to choose when, with whom, in what way, and how often they procreate. This includes a moral freedom not to have children, even if one could (at comparatively little cost to oneself) create people whose lives were extremely worth living (Mulgan, 2006, pp. 134–5).
3 **Moderate Obligations:** Parents' obligations to their children are much stronger than their obligations to strangers – and even to close friends or other relatives. But parents also enjoy broad moral freedom to raise their children as they see fit, and there is no overriding obligation to maximise the quality of one's child's life.
4 **Liberal Population Policy:** There is no exact 'optimal' population size, and the population can be kept within desirable upper and lower bounds by social policy incentives and nudges rather than by legal, social, or moral coercion.

This collective utilitarian defence of procreative freedom is inspired by Hooker's observation that rule utilitarianism's question is not 'What if everyone did that?' but rather 'What if everyone felt free to do that?' Hooker puts the point well:

Suppose my nephew tells me he refuses to have children. If everyone refuses to have children, the human species will die out. This would be a disastrous consequence. But it is irrelevant to the morality of my nephew's decision. What is relevant is that everyone's feeling free not to have children will not lead to the extinction of the species. Plenty of people who do not feel obligated to have children nevertheless *want* to – and, if free to do so, will. Thus, there is no need for a moral obligation to have children. Neither is there any need for a general moral obligation to have heterosexual intercourse. (Hooker, 2000, p. 177.)

In *Future People*, I concluded that our ideal moral outlook will include something analogous to the following moral principle:

The Flexible Lexical Rule. Reproduce if and only if you want to, so long as you are *reasonably sure* that your child will enjoy a life above the lexical level, and *very sure* that the risk of your child falling below the zero level is *very small*. (Mulgan, 2006, p. 174.)

This formulation is very vague. Much turns on the interpretation of the italicised phrases. However, as Hooker argues, such vagueness is a strength, not a weakness: 'Rule Consequentialists are as aware as anyone that figuring out whether a rule applies can require not merely attention to detail, but also sensitivity, imagination, interpretation, and judgement.' (Hooker, 2000, p. 88.)

As I argued in section 4.1, the context-dependence of its lexical level gives ideal outlook utilitarianism the flexibility to survive the transition to a *broken world*. Any liberal procreative ethic is especially vulnerable in broken futures. On the one hand, too much procreative freedom might push the population beyond what is sustainable given the scarce and fluctuating resources of a broken future. On the other hand, if reproduction becomes too burdensome or the prospects for one's own children seem too bleak, then a liberal moral outlook where *everyone* has the moral option of *not procreating at all* might usher in immediate human extinction by producing a second generation that is unsustainably small. Non-utilitarian liberals struggle to make sense of this transition. By contrast, ideal outlook utilitarianism adapts to new circumstances, as its ideal moral outlook includes an underlying disposition to re-interpret or re-imagine one's moral commitments to ensure that human civilisation continues. In particular, future utilitarians might respond to a broken future by revising their notion of a lexical level or introducing a new obligation to procreate when the survival of humanity is at stake.

4.5 Uncertainty: Empirical and Normative

Opponents have long objected that utilitarianism is morally *clueless*. Because it makes rightness depend on facts we could never know, utilitarianism cannot offer any useful advice (Lenman, 2000). The effects of my present actions will ramify through the generations in ways that I cannot possibly guess. If I never know what will produce the best consequences, I can never know what I should do. While cluelessness is a general problem for all consequentialists, an intergenerational focus clearly exacerbates it. The more we acknowledge the full range of possible futures, the harder it is to believe that we can predict anything.

Collective utilitarianism seems to exacerbate our cluelessness. If we can't predict the consequences of a single act, how can we hope to calculate the long-term results of the *widespread internalisation* of rules? One preliminary reply is that our interest in ideal codes or outlooks is derivative. We use these ideals to tell us how to act *in our particular present situation*. For that purpose, we often don't need to uncover all the details of the ideal code or outlook. It is sufficient to know that, whatever its other features might be, the best moral outlook will offer *this advice here and now*. For instance, we could be confident that anyone who had internalised the ideal moral outlook would refrain from gratuitous torture, even if we didn't know exactly what else such a person would think or do. However, this brief reply is unlikely to remove all our worries about cluelessness. Can utilitarians do better?

As we saw in our discussion of virtual and digital futures, our uncertainty is often *normative* as well as empirical. We want to promote value, but we don't know what things are valuable. I argued in section 3.4 that credible virtual futures provide a decisive argument for the objective list theory over both hedonism and preference theory. This claim is very controversial. What is *not* controversial is that the three competing accounts of well-being *disagree* about virtual futures. Hedonists and preference theorists accept the virtual future on its own terms, arguing that the pleasures and preference-satisfactions it offers constitute the only *real* human goods. On these views of well-being, the choice between broken and virtual futures is simply a choice between brokenness and post-scarcity. And *that* choice is a trivial one. By contrast, objective list theorists who attach inherent value to connections with the non-human natural world will find virtual futures very deficient. We saw in section 3.5 that *digital* futures raise analogous problems involving both metaphysical and normative uncertainty. Are digital beings conscious? And how much does this matter? Is the digital future a valueless void, a broken world, or a post-scarcity paradise?

If we cannot decide between hedonism, preference theory, and objective list theory, then we cannot decide whether or not virtual and digital futures are desirable. If we teach the next generation to be thoroughgoing hedonists, they will embrace the virtual future without regret, thus maximising both pleasure and preference satisfaction. This is unproblematic if hedonism or preference theory is correct. But what if both theories are wrong?

Utilitarians have five general options when confronted by any disputed question about value.

1 **Conditional/Disjunctive:** Utilitarianism offers (only) a series of conditional claims about what we should do. If x1 is the correct account of value (or if you value x1), then you should do A1; If x2 is the correct account of value (or if you value x2), then you should do A2; etc.

2 **Exclusivist:** Utilitarians should select our favourite account of value and then ask what best promotes it. We can separate two varieties of exclusivism:
   a. **Partisan Exclusivism:** I concede that I cannot demonstrate the superiority of my preferred account of well-being, but I incorporate that account into my utilitarian theory because (a) it strikes me as the most plausible and (b) I hope that enough readers will agree with me.
   b. **Ambitious Exclusivism:** I claim that I *can* demonstrate that my preferred account of well-being *is* the correct account.

3 **Agnostic:** Our real interest, as utilitarians, is in what we should *do*, not in questions of value for their own sake. Sometimes we can determine that some particular act, rule, or moral outlook best promotes value even if we cannot agree about what value *is*. The separation between utilitarianism and consequentialism in contemporary moral philosophy often reflects this kind of agnosticism. In the literature on aggregation, for instance, most contributors adopt Parfit's deliberately place-holding term 'whatever makes life worth living' (Parfit, 1984). This is because they assume that debates about how to respond to or aggregate well-being are independent of the details of what well-being *is*.

4 **Prospectivism:** Utilitarians should treat uncertainty about value in the same way as any other uncertainty – we assign probabilities to different accounts of value and then choose the option the offers the greatest expected value (Zimmerman, 2014).

5 **Maximin:** Utilitarians should play it safe, selecting the option that guarantees the least bad outcome *even if the least favourable value theory turns out to be true*.

The many uncertainties introduced by virtual and digital futures are philosophically significant because they undermine all of these standard responses to uncertainty. To reliably promote well-being, we need a moral outlook that works across all credible futures. Once virtual futures enter the picture, it makes a huge difference *what* we seek to maximise. It really matters whether pleasure and preference-satisfaction are all that is good for people. We can no longer remain agnostic, assuming that the same moral outlook will maximise pleasure *and* preference-satisfaction *and* objective goods. On the other hand, it would be reckless, given our philosophical uncertainty, to select one account of well-being and simply seek to maximise *that*. If we select the wrong account, our 'ideal' moral outlook could be very sub-optimal indeed. Although it is less extreme, prospectivism also seems too risky, for the same reason. (Suppose an unconscious digital future offers high expected value but a non-negligible risk of annihilating value altogether. Should responsible utilitarians take this risk?) Finally, while it sidesteps this worry, maximin fails because different moral views disagree about what counts as the worst outcome. (Is an empty world better or worse than a world where everyone suffers?)

A more ambitious collective utilitarian response to both empirical and normative uncertainty appeals to moral progress and moral imaginativeness. Moral imaginativeness is the ability to think more deeply about the nature of value and morality and to imagine new moral norms suited to various possible futures (Mulgan, 2017, 2018c). In our culture, this task is largely confined to speculative fiction. It has not been prominent in moral philosophy. In utilitarian future ethics, by contrast, imaginative moral experiments in living (to adapt a phrase from J. S. Mill) will be essential elements in everyone's moral repertoire.

We need moral imaginativeness because we are multiply uncertain about the future. Our ignorance has three overlapping dimensions: empirical, metaphysical, and evaluative. We don't know what will happen, we don't know what the world is ultimately like, and we don't know what really matters.

Our goal is to identify the ideal moral outlook without first resolving our uncertainty about well-being or metaphysics. One possible solution appeals to the idea of *moral progress*. Suppose we agree that we *could* produce a next generation whose moral sensitivity and moral imaginativeness were significantly greater than our own, and whose judgements about value and well-being were much more finely nuanced than ours. If we teach a moral outlook that emphasises moral imaginativeness, we can reasonably expect to produce a next generation of (comparative) moral experts.

This hypothetical claim about moral progress should be uncontroversial. Collectively, we could surely enhance moral imaginativeness. After all, we know that experts of all kinds are created by education. And if we *cannot* influence future moral outlooks for the better, then this would be a fatal blow, not merely for rule or ideal outlook utilitarianism but for any systematic future ethic.

On the other hand, if we *can* count on the next generation's superior moral judgement, then we can use that judgement to sidestep our own uncertainty about value. The trick is to delegate *to them* the difficult business of deciding what the ideal outlook should be maximising in the first place! Instead of teaching the next generation to do X or avoid Y (on the grounds that these rules maximise, say, pleasure), we should encourage them to first develop their moral imaginativeness and then to pursue whatever *they* judge to be most valuable. Because of their superior moral and epistemic position, we can be reasonably confident that a moral outlook that emphasises imaginativeness and judgement will more reliably promote well-being than any similar outlook that doesn't emphasise those things, even if we don't ourselves know what well-being is. If we want to embody the ideal moral outlook in our own lives, then we should start by making our own imaginative moral experiments and trying to imagine the ethics of the future.

4.6 Human Extinction

Recent technological and environmental threats have focused philosophical attention on the very real possibility of imminent human extinction. Most people agree that it would be a very bad thing for humanity to become extinct too soon. Utilitarianism offers a clear explanation for this conviction. If we are confident that future human lives would, on balance, be worth living, then human extinction involves not only the suffering and death of billions of actual people but also the loss of a much larger number of happy future lives. For utilitarians, the *loss* of all that future human happiness – the *absence* of all those happy future people – is the worst thing about human extinction.[15]

Throughout his philosophical career, Derek Parfit used the possibility that human history may be only just beginning to highlight the moral significance of potential catastrophes threatening human survival. Parfit's various reflections are worth quoting at length, as they introduce the central themes of recent utilitarian reflection on human extinction.

> I believe that if we destroy mankind, as we now could, this outcome would be *much* worse that most people think. . . . The Earth will remain inhabitable for at least another two billion years. Civilization began only a few thousand years ago. If we do not destroy mankind, these few thousand years may be only a tiny fraction of the whole of civilized human history. The difference between [a nuclear war that kills 99 per cent of the world's existing population] and [a nuclear war that kills 100 per cent] may thus be the difference between this tiny fraction and all of the rest of this history. (Parfit, 1984, p. 453.)

> If we act wisely in the next few centuries, humanity will survive its most dangerous and decisive period. Our descendants could, if necessary, go elsewhere, spreading through the galaxy. (Parfit, 2011, vol. 2, p. 616.)

---

[15] I explore the issues sketched in this section at greater length in Mulgan, 2018d, 2019 and forthcoming a.

What now matters most is that we avoid ending human history. If there are no rational beings elsewhere, it may depend on us and our successors whether it will all be worth it, because the existence of the Universe will have been on the whole good. (Parfit, 2011, vol. 2, p. 620.)

Given what our successors could achieve in the next million or billion years, here and elsewhere in our galaxy, it would be likely to be very much worse if there were no future people. (Parfit, 2017, pp. 118–19.)

Parfit's sentiments are echoed by other contemporary moral philosophers:

Most of us believe that human extinction would be the worst of those possible tragedies that have more than a negligible probability of actually occurring. (McMahan, 2013, p. 26.)

Surely, if we developed a pill enabling each of us to live wonderful lives for 120 years it would be terrible for us to take the pill if the cost of doing so were the extinction of humanity. (Temkin, 2012, p. 414.[16])

Similar thoughts have led some utilitarians to argue that existential threats to humanity should dominate our ethical thinking (e.g., Beckstead, 2013). The basic idea behind such *dominance reasoning* is simple:

1 If we avoid imminent human extinction, humanity could continue for billions of years.
2 The expected value of possible futures where humanity continues for billions of years is astronomically large.
3 Therefore, the expected value of *any reduction in the probability of* imminent human extinction is also astronomically large.
4 Therefore, any reduction in the probability of imminent human extinction outweighs any present or near future cost.

Dominance reasoning applies to both individual and collective utilitarianism (Kaczmarek, 2017). If dominance reasoning is correct, then the moral outlook that maximises expected future well-being must minimise the risk of imminent human extinction. It is then tempting to conclude that anyone who has internalised that ideal moral outlook must give *lexical* priority to extinction risk reduction.

Accepting dominance reasoning could have radical implications for utilitarian future ethics. As Parfit observed, the *very long-term* survival of humanity depends on escaping our dependence on the Earth and colonising the galaxy. Dominance reasoning says that we must devote all our efforts to launching this

---

[16] Temkin adds a footnote that this claim 'is almost as obvious as any claim can be in the normative domain' (Temkin, 2012, p. 414).

process of colonisation as soon as possible. This would be *very* expensive –
greatly depleting non-renewable resources, causing enormous environmental
damage, and making life much less pleasant for those remaining on Earth. If
extinction risk reduction has *lexical* priority over all other human concerns, then
present and near-future people may end up paying a very high price to secure the
long-term human future.

Does utilitarianism demand that we do *whatever it takes* to reduce the risk of
imminent human extinction? I argued in section 2 that utilitarian ethics should
be future-directed, collective, and take account of the full range of possible
futures. Our ideal moral outlook will certainly pay particular attention to issues
surrounding human extinction, galactic colonisation, and other distant future
threats. However, it is not obvious that utilitarians must give lexical priority to
avoiding imminent human extinction. I end our exploration of utilitarian future
ethics by briefly sketching a number of ways that utilitarians might limit the
force of dominance reasoning.

Our first two limitations are specific to *collective* utilitarianism:

1 **General limits on demandingness:** As we saw in section 2.2, one central
   argument for collective utilitarianism is that it is less demanding than act
   utilitarianism. The need for widespread internalisation within a *human*
   population prevents our ideal moral outlook from making demands that
   are too extreme. (On the other hand, we also saw in sections 2.2 and 2.3 that
   the ideal outlook can still be *very* demanding compared to non-utilitarian
   morality!)

2 **Consequences in other possible futures:** Collective utilitarians assess
   moral outlooks against the full range of possible futures. While it might
   produce the best consequences in some cases, a single-minded concentration
   on human extinction could also have very undesirable consequences if
   humanity faces other (more probable) threats. Most obviously, the fantasy
   of avoiding the consequences of our own environmental destruction by
   escaping into space could prove disastrous if galactic colonisation is never
   actually feasible and our descendants realise this only when it is too late to
   save the Earth.

Both individual and collective utilitarians can also question a number of
empirical and evaluative claims underpinning dominance reasoning.

3 **How likely is long-term survival?** Dominance reasoning promises an
   astronomically valuable human future. But what if that future is also *astronomically unlikely*? Recorded human history stretches back a few thousand
   years. Modern technological industrial civilisation is only a few hundred

years old. How plausible is the suggestion that, even if we survive the next few centuries, humanity will then survive for another ten thousand years – let alone a *billion*? Dominance reasoning assumes that the largeness of the relevant pay-off *dwarfs* the smallness of the corresponding probability. But perhaps this difference merely reflects our limited human imaginations: we find it easier to imagine astronomically large numbers of people than astronomically small probabilities.

Dominance reasoning faces an obvious dilemma. Imminent extinction is on the public agenda because (a) there is a non-negligible probability that humanity will go extinct *in the next two centuries*. We are then asked to believe that (b) the cumulative probability that humanity would survive *for the following ten million centuries* is *not* astronomically small. These two claims are in tension. If the probability of extinction during *any given future century* is non-negligible, then the probability of *avoiding* extinction for each of ten million centuries *is* astronomically small. The two claims (a) and (b) are therefore only compatible if some very special feature of the next two centuries means that the risk of extinction is *much higher* now than in the far distant future. Why is *this* humanity's 'most dangerous and decisive period'? (Parfit, 2011, vol. 2, p. 616.) The standard answer is that '[o]ur descendants could, if necessary, go elsewhere, spreading through the galaxy' (Parfit, 2011, vol. 2, p. 616.) thereby very greatly reducing the ongoing threat of extinction. But is this just another failure of imagination? Are we simply too ignorant to appreciate the *new threats* that might confront any space-faring civilisation? (Consider a sobering analogy. Our distant ancestors might have hoped to remove the threat of extinction by spreading across the entire globe. But this has simply opened up new *global* extinction threats.)

4 **Beyond totalism:** Dominance reasoning works best if we assume totalism. It is only *astronomically* valuable to add an astronomical number of (happy) human lives if each extra life increases total value. However, as we saw in section 4.1, totalism is a minority position even within the utilitarian tradition. The most popular alternatives – notably averagism – are not nearly as susceptible to dominance reasoning, because they do not attach astronomically high value to futures where humanity survives for billions of years.

5 **Will the distant human future be desirable?** For any *utilitarian*, it is only desirable to avoid imminent human extinction if (most) far distant future lives are *worth living*. Dominance reasoning typically presumes a predominantly happy human future. Yet virtually all utilitarians agree that some *actual* (past and present) lives are not worth living. As Parfit himself noted, pessimists have always argued that human life is not (on balance) worth living. The far distant human future could be negative rather

than positive. The presumption of a happy future remains controversial. Are most *present* lives worth living? Have most *past* human lives been worth living? If not, why assume the future will be better? Can we reasonably project current levels of happiness or current (upward) trends indefinitely into the future?

6 **Is dominance reasoning anthropocentric?** Dominance reasoning sidelines *future non-human animals*. Many threats to humanity also threaten other terrestrial species. However, the interests of humans and non-humans could come apart. First, *human* extinction might not involve the extinction of *all* sentient beings – and future non-human welfare could then itself be astronomical. Second, the demise of humanity might be good news for many other sentient species. Our exit might raise future well-being. Third, depleting terrestrial resources to fuel *human* colonisation of the galaxy could greatly reduce future non-human well-being. Utilitarians who accord equal value to the welfare of *all* future sentient beings may judge that the human payoff is not worth the non-human cost.

7 **Is dominance reasoning terra-centric?** Dominance reasoning ignores *future extraterrestrial well-being*. Human galactic colonisation poses an unknown threat to any as-yet-undiscovered sentient extraterrestrial life that our descendants might encounter. 'Successful' human colonisation might reduce *total galactic well-being* – perhaps to an astronomical degree. (For instance, we might inadvertently prevent the emergence of some future sentient species whose happiness would have dwarfed any feasible human future.) Parfit argues that if we are alone in the universe, then human survival has the utmost importance. But what if we are not alone?

8 **Should we obsess about outlier cases?** Dominance reasoning privileges policies that feature a very high positive payoff with a very low probability. Utilitarian moral philosophers can reasonably reject this notorious implication of expected utility maximisation. Perhaps the morally appropriate response to uncertainty is more risk-averse. (To take a stark example: even if we embrace totalism, would we really consider it *morally admirable* to accept a gamble that offered a 51 per cent chance of doubling future human happiness alongside a 49 per cent chance of annihilating humanity?)

9 **Is human extinction the worst possibility?** In response to the previous objection, proponents of dominance reasoning will argue that *risk-averse* utilitarians should be *especially* worried about human extinction. Surely the early end of the human story represents the worst possible result! However, this is too optimistic. Just as there are some individual fates that are worse than death, so too there are some possible futures that are worse – from a utilitarian point of view – than futures where humanity becomes extinct

very soon. We can easily imagine a vast range of *very broken futures* where total and average well-being (for humans, animals, or extraterrestrials) falls well below zero. If we succeed in avoiding imminent human extinction, then we also raise the probability of these especially undesirable futures. And while such grim futures may not be very likely, they are not obviously astronomically improbable.

I conclude that while utilitarian future ethics certainly has reason to think hard about issues surrounding human extinction, it is not yet clear where that thinking will lead.

5 Concluding Remarks

Any adequate ethical theory must confront the unprecedented ethical challenges of our Anthropocene Era. I have argued that, while utilitarianism is uniquely well-equipped to meet those challenges, the need to adapt to different possible futures will force utilitarians to develop their theory in new directions. Utilitarian future ethics requires an objective account of well-being and a collective scope. Many important questions remain, and much depends on the precise details of the new challenges and circumstances that future utilitarians will actually face. What should future utilitarians include in this list of essential components of a good human life? How should they balance different human goods, especially in futures where resources are scarce? Should utilitarians retain a focus on total utility or retreat to less ambitious theories of aggregation? How should utilitarians incorporate non-humans – animals, virtual avatars, digital beings, extraterrestrials – into their accounts of well-being and aggregation? How should utilitarians combine different foci of evaluation: direct and indirect, individual and collective? How should utilitarians think about human extinction and the distant future?

Our exploration of utilitarian future ethics has delivered more questions than answers. But this too is in keeping with the open-ended empiricism of the utilitarian tradition.

References

Anscombe, G. E. M. (1957). Modern moral philosophy. *Philosophy*, **23**, 1–19.

Arrhenius, G. (forthcoming). *Population Ethics*, Oxford: Oxford University Press.

Attfield, R. (2009). Mediated responsibilities, global warming, and the scope of ethics. *Journal of Social Philosophy*, **40**, 225–36.

Baier, K. (1958). *The Moral Point of View*, Ithaca, NY: Cornell University Press.

Beckstead, N. (2013). On the overwhelming importance of shaping the far future, Rutgers PhD thesis.

Bentham, J. (1838). *The Works of Jeremy Bentham*, ed. J. Bowring, Edinburgh: William Tait.

Bentham, J. (1996). *An Introduction to the Principles of Morals and Legislation*, eds., J. H. Burns and H. L. A. Hart, Oxford: Oxford University Press.

Blackford, R. and Broderick, D. (2014). *Intelligence Unbound: The Future of Uploaded and Machine Minds*, Oxford: Wiley-Blackwell.

Bostrom, N. (2014). *Superintelligence: Paths, Dangers, Strategies*, Oxford: Oxford University Press.

Bradley, B. (2014). Objective theories of well-being. In B. Eggleston and D. E. Miller, eds., *The Cambridge Companion to Utilitarianism*, Cambridge: Cambridge University Press, pp. 199–215.

Broome, J. (2004). *Weighing Lives*, Oxford: Oxford University Press.

Bykvist, K. (2009). *Utilitarianism: A Guide for the Perplexed*, London: Continuum.

Chappell, R. (2017). Rethinking the asymmetry. *Canadian Journal of Philosophy*, **47**, 166–77.

Cowen, T. and Parfit, D. (1992). Against the social discount rate. In P. Laslett and J. Fishkin, eds., *Justice between Age Groups and Generations*, New Haven: Yale University Press, pp. 144–61.

Crisp, R. (2006). *Reasons and the Good*, Oxford: Oxford University Press.

Crisp, R. (2015). Well-Being. *The Stanford Encyclopaedia of Philosophy* (Summer 2015 edition), Edward N. Zalta (ed.), http://plato.stanford.edu/archives/sum2015/entries/well-being.

de Lazari-Radek, K. and Singer, P. (2017). *Utilitarianism: A Very Short Introduction*, Oxford: Oxford University Press.

Dorsey, D. (2012). Subjectivism without desire. *The Philosophical Review*, **121**, 407–42.

Driver, J. (2014). Global utilitarianism. In B. Eggleston and D. E. Miller, eds., *The Cambridge Companion to Utilitarianism*, Cambridge: Cambridge University Press, pp. 150–9.

Eggleston, B. (2014). Act utilitarianism. In B. Eggleston and D. E. Miller, eds., *The Cambridge Companion to Utilitarianism*, Cambridge: Cambridge University Press, pp. 114–31.

Eggleston, B. and Miller, D. E. eds. (2014). *The Cambridge Companion to Utilitarianism*, Cambridge: Cambridge University Press.

Feldman, F. (2011). What we learn from the experience machine. In R. M. Bader and J. Meadowcroft, eds., *The Cambridge Companion to Nozick's Anarchy, State, and Utopia*, Cambridge: Cambridge University Press, pp. 59–86.

Finnis, J. (1980). *Natural Law and Natural Rights*, Oxford: Oxford University Press.

Fletcher, G. (2013). A fresh start for the objective-list theory of well-being. *Utilitas*, **25**, 206–20.

Floridi, L. (2014). *The Fourth Revolution: How the infosphere is reshaping human reality*, Oxford: Oxford University Press.

Gosseries, A. and Meyer, L., eds. (2009). *Intergenerational Justice*, Oxford: Oxford University Press.

Greaves, H. (2017). Population Axiology. *Philosophy Compass*, **12**, online early: https://doi.org/10.1111/phc3.12442

Griffin, J. (1986). *Well-Being*, Oxford: Oxford University Press.

Hanson, R. (2016). *The Age of EM*, Oxford: Oxford University Press.

Hare, R. M. (1982). *Moral Thinking*, Oxford: Oxford University Press.

Hauskeller, M. (2013). *Better Humans? Understanding the Enhancement Project*, Durham: Acumen.

Heathwood, C. (2014). Subjective theories of well-being. In B. Eggleston and D. E. Miller, eds., *The Cambridge Companion to Utilitarianism*, Cambridge: Cambridge University Press, pp. 180–98.

Heyd, D. (1992). *Genethics: Moral Issues in the Creation of People*, Berkeley, CA: University of California Press.

Hofstadter, D. (2007). *I Am a Strange Loop*, New York: Basic Books.

Holtug, N. (2010). *Persons, Interests, and Justice*, Oxford: Oxford University Press.

Hooker, B. (2000). *Ideal Code, Real World*, Oxford: Oxford University Press.

Hooker, B. (2008). Variable 'versus' fixed-rate rule-utilitarianism. *Philosophical Quarterly*, **58**, 344–52.

Jackson, F. (1999). *From Metaphysics to Ethics*, Oxford: Oxford University Press.

Kaczmarek, P. (2017). How much is rule-consequentialism really willing to give up to save the future of humanity? *Utilitas*, **29**, 239–249.

Kavka, G. (1982). The paradox of future individuals. *Philosophy and Public Affairs*, **11**, 93–112.

Lenman, J. (2000). Consequentialism and cluelessness. *Philosophy and Public Affairs*, **29**, 342–70.

McMahan, J. (2013). Causing people to exist and saving people's lives. *Journal of Ethics*, **17**, 5–35.

Mill, J. S. (1963). *The Collected Works of John Stuart Mill*, ed. J. M. Robson, 33 vols., Toronto: University of Toronto Press.

Miller, D. E. (2014). Rule utilitarianism. In B. Eggleston and D. E. Miller, eds., *The Cambridge Companion to Utilitarianism*, Cambridge: Cambridge University Press, 132–49.

Mulgan, T. (2001). *The Demands of Consequentialism*, Oxford: Oxford University Press.

Mulgan, T. (2002). The Reverse Repugnant Conclusion. *Utilitas*, **14**, 360–4.

Mulgan, T. (2004). Two Parfit puzzles. In J. Ryberg and R. Tannsjo, eds., *The Repugnant Conclusion: Essays on Population Ethics*, Dordrecht: Kluwer Academic Publishers, pp. 23–45.

Mulgan, T. (2006). *Future People*, Oxford: Oxford University Press.

Mulgan, T. (2007). *Understanding Utilitarianism*, Durham: Acumen.

Mulgan, T. (2011). *Ethics for a Broken World: Reimagining Philosophy after Catastrophe*, Durham: Acumen.

Mulgan, T. (2014). Ethics for possible futures. *Proceedings of the Aristotelian Society*, **114**, 57–73.

Mulgan, T. (2015a). Utilitarianism for a broken world. *Utilitas*, **27**, 92–114.

Mulgan, T. (2015b). Mill and the broken world. *Revue Internationale de Philosophie*, **69**, 205–24.

Mulgan, T. (2015c). Theory and intuition in a broken world. In S.-G. Chappell, ed., *Intuition, Theory, and Anti-theory*, Oxford: Oxford University Press, pp. 141–66.

Mulgan, T. (2016). Theorising about justice for a broken world. In K. Watene and J. Drydyk, eds., *Theorizing Justice: Crucial Insights and Future Directions*, London: Rowman & Littlefield, pp. 15–32.

Mulgan, T. (2017). How should utilitarians think about the future? *Canadian Journal of Philosophy*, **47**, 290–312.

Mulgan, T. (2018a). Answering to future people. *Journal of Applied Philosophy*, **35**, 532–48.

Mulgan, T. (2018b). Moral imaginativeness, moral creativity and possible futures. In B. Gaut and M. Kieran, eds., *Creativity and Philosophy*, New York: Routledge, pp. 350–68.

Mulgan, T. (2018c). Can liberal rule consequentialism survive threats of human extinction? Paper presented to workshop at Southampton University, September 2018.

Mulgan, T. (2019a). Corporate agency and possible futures. *Journal of Business Ethics*, **154**, 901–916.

Mulgan, T. (2019b). What is really wrong with human extinction? In C. Schmidt-Petri and M. Schefczyk, eds., *Proceedings of the International Society for Utilitarian Studies*, Karlsruhe, Germany: KIT Scientific Publishing.

Mulgan, T. (forthcoming a). *Future Worlds: The Moral Significance of Generation Starships*. Draft manuscript.

Mulgan, T. (forthcoming b). *Moral Philosophy, Superintelligence, and the Singularity*. Draft manuscript.

Narveson, J. (1967) Utilitarianism and new generations. *Mind*, **76**, 62–72.

Nordhaus, W. (2007). *The Challenge of Global Warming: Economic Models and Environmental Policy*, available at www.econ.yale.edu/~nordhaus/home page/OldWebFiles/DICEGAMS/dice_mss_072407_all.pdf.

Nozick, R. (1974). *Anarchy, State, and Utopia*, New York: Blackwells.

Parfit, D. (1984). *Reasons and Persons*, Oxford: Oxford University Press.

Parfit, D. (1986). Overpopulation and the quality of life. In P. Singer, ed., *Applied Ethics*, Oxford: Oxford University Press, pp. 145–64.

Parfit, D. (1991). Equality or priority. The Lindley Lecture, University of Kansas.

Parfit, D. (2011). *On What Matters*, Oxford: Oxford University Press.

Parfit, D. (2017). Future people, the non-identity problem, and person-affecting principles. *Philosophy and Public Affairs*, **45**, 118–57.

Rawls, J. (1971). *A Theory of Justice*, Cambridge, MA: Harvard University Press.

Ridge, M. (2006). Introducing variable-rate rule-utilitarianism. *Philosophical Quarterly*, **56**, 242–53.

Roberts, M. (2002). A new way of doing the best we can: person-based consequentialism and the equality problem. *Ethics*, **112**, 315–50.

Roberts, M. (2011). The asymmetry: a solution. *Theoria*, **77**, 333–67.

Roberts, M. (2007). The non-identity fallacy: harm, probability and another look at Parfit's depletion example. *Utilitas*, **19**, 267–311.

Ryberg, J. and Tannsjo, T., eds. (2004). *The Repugnant Conclusion: Essays on Population Ethics*, Dordrecht: Kluwer.

Schultz, B. (2017). *The Happiness Philosophers: The Lives and Works of the Great Utilitarians*, Princeton, NJ: Princeton University Press.

Searle, J. (1997). *The Mystery of Consciousness*, London: Granta.

Shaw, W. (1999). *Contemporary Ethics: Taking Account of Utilitarianism*, Oxford: Blackwell.

Sidgwick, H. (1907). *The Methods of Ethics*, London: Macmillan.

Singer, P. (1972). Famine, affluence and morality. *Philosophy and Public Affairs*, **1**, 229–43.

Singer, P. (1975). *Animal Liberation*, New York: Harper Collins.

Singer, P. (2011). *Practical Ethics*, 3rd edn., Cambridge: Cambridge University Press.

Sinnott-Armstrong, W. (2005). It's not *my* fault: global warming and individual moral obligations. In W. Sinnott-Armstrong, and R. B. Howarth, eds., *Perspectives on Climate Change: Science, Economics, Politics, Ethics*, Amsterdam: Elsevier, pp. 293–315.

Smith, H. (2010). Measuring the consequences of rules. *Utilitas*, **22**, 413–33.

Stern, N. (2006). *Stern Review: The Economics of Climate Change*, at http://webarchive.nationalarchives.gov.uk/+

Stross, C. (2005). *Singularity Sky*, London: Orbit.

Temkin, L. S. (2012). *Rethinking the Good*, Oxford: Oxford University Press.

Thomson, J. (1976). Killing, letting die, and the trolley problem. *The Monist*, **59**, 204–17.

Valberg, J. J. (2007). *Dream, Death, and the Self*, Princeton, NJ: Princeton University Press.

Woodard, C. (2013). Classifying theories of welfare. *Philosophical Studies*, **165**, 787–803.

Zimmerman, M. (2014). *Ignorance and Moral Obligation*, Oxford: Oxford University Press.

Cambridge Elements ≡

Elements in Ethics

Ben Eggleston
University of Kansas

Ben Eggleston is a professor of philosophy at the University of Kansas. He is the editor of John Stuart Mill, *Utilitarianism: With Related Remarks from Mill's Other Writings* (Hackett, 2017) and a co-editor of *Moral Theory and Climate Change: Ethical Perspectives on a Warming Planet* (Routledge, 2020), *The Cambridge Companion to Utilitarianism* (Cambridge, 2014), and *John Stuart Mill and the Art of Life* (Oxford, 2011). He is also the author of numerous articles and book chapters on various topics in ethics.

Dale E. Miller
Old Dominion University, Virginia

Dale E. Miller is a professor of philosophy at Old Dominion University. He is the author of *John Stuart Mill: Moral, Social and Political Thought* (Polity, 2010) and a co-editor of *Moral Theory and Climate Change: Ethical Perspectives on a Warming Planet* (Routledge, 2020), *A Companion to Mill* (Blackwell, 2017), *The Cambridge Companion to Utilitarianism* (Cambridge, 2014), *John Stuart Mill and the Art of Life* (Oxford, 2011), and *Morality, Rules, and Consequences: A Critical Reader* (Edinburgh, 2000). He is also the editor-in-chief of *Utilitas* and the author of numerous articles and book chapters on various topics in ethics broadly construed.

About the Series

This Elements series provides an extensive overview of major figures, theories, and concepts in the field of ethics. Each entry in the series acquaints students with the main aspects of its topic while articulating the author's distinctive viewpoint in a manner that will interest researchers.

Cambridge Elements$^{\equiv}$

Elements in Ethics

Made in the USA
Monee, IL
22 August 2024

64399631R00046